GCSE ENGLISH
FOR EDEXCEL
REVISION BOOK

ANDREW LIDDLE

RICHARD ORMROD

SHIRLEY ORMROD

Hodder Murray
A MEMBER OF THE HODDER HEADLINE GROUP

Acknowledgements

The authors and publisher would like to thank the following for their kind permission to reproduce copyright material:

Copyright text:
p21 'Should it be a crime to hit your child?' by Kamal Ahmed © The *Observer*; p22 'Discipline Tips that Guide Children to Better Behavior' © Deborah Critzer-Fox, *Positive Parenting Newsletter*, www.positiveparenting.com; p32 'whowhatwhenwherewhy' by Clare Coulson © Telegraph Group Ltd 2003; p33 '208mph: In the tracks of Rocket and Mallard, Eurostar breaks British record' by Paul Marston © Telegraph Group Ltd 2003; p37 *Street Scape 2003* leaflet: photograph © Rachel Henson and Pearshape; text © Arts Services, Portsmouth City Council; design © Printcraft (Southsea) Ltd.

Copyright photographs:
p9 *Hunting Red Fox* © W. Perry Conway/CORBIS; p15 *Cathy O'Dowd* © Blnod Joshi/AP Photo; p33 *George Stephenson's Rocket* © The Science Museum; p33 *Flying Scotsman Leaving King's Cross Station* © Hulton-Deutsch Collection/CORBIS; p33 *Steam Engine 'Mallard' Travels Along Tracks* © Graham Howden, Cordaiy Photo Library Ltd./CORBIS; p33 *Eurostar Breaks Speed Record* © Gareth Fuller/PA Photos Ltd.

Copyright artwork:
pp5, 14 and 73 © Oxford Designers and Illustrators.

Every effort has been made to trace copyright holders of material reproduced in this book. Any rights not acknowledged here will be acknowledged in subsequent printings if notice is given to the publisher.

Note about the Internet links in the book. The user should be aware that URLs or web addresses change regularly. Every effort has been made to ensure the accuracy of the URLs provided in this book on going to press. It is inevitable, however, that some will change. It is sometimes possible to find a relocated web page by just typing in the address of the home page for a website in the URL window of your browser.

Orders: please contact Bookpoint Ltd, 130 Milton Park, Abingdon, Oxon OX14 4SB. Telephone: (44) 01235 827720. Fax: (44) 01235 400454. Lines are open from 9.00–6.00, Monday to Saturday, with a 24 hour message answering service. You can also order through our website: www.hoddereducation.co.uk

British Library Cataloguing in Publication Data
A catalogue record for this title is available from the British Library

ISBN -10: 0 340 81488 8
ISBN -13: 978 0 340 81488 8

First Published 2004
Impression number   10 9 8 7 6 5 4
Year   2010 2009 2008 2007 2006 2005

Copyright © 2004 Andrew Liddle, Richard Ormrod and Shirley Ormrod

Hodder Headline's policy is to use papers that are natural, renewable and recyclable products and made from wood grown in sustainable forests. The logging and manufacturing processes are expected to conform to the enviromental regulations of the country of origin.

Typeset by Fakenham Photosetting Limited, Fakenham, Norfolk.
Printed in Great Britain for Hodder Murray, a division of Hodder Education , 338 Euston Road, London NW1 3BH by Hobbs the Printers Ltd, Hampshire.

CONTENTS

Dear Student,

This revision guide is your passport to GCSE success in both English and English Literature. It has been written to go with the approved textbook, *GCSE English for Edexcel*, and is a vital aid to your revision.

Importantly, it is a self-tutor – one you can work through without the aid of a teacher – and it contains top tips from examiners that will help you not just to pass but to seriously improve your grades.

For best results, we recommend you actively work through as many of the tasks as possible. Be sure not to waste time looking at sections you have not opted to take in the exams, though.

We suggest you complete the task boxes as fully as possible. They're designed:

✱ to refamiliarise you with the set texts and tasks

✱ to reinforce the key skills

✱ to give you a firm grasp of the necessary terminology.

Do as many of the assignments and written tasks as possible, taking no more than 40 minutes on each.

By the time you have worked through the guide, you will be raring to get stuck into those exams.

Good luck!

What Do the Grades Really Mean?

A*	Work is original, sophisticated, perceptive, and analytical; its clear, penetrating argument is based on strong evidence; it is fully engaged with the text/task; and has a controlled, fluent style, a wide and rich vocabulary.
A	Full, organised, relevant, persuasive and clear; based on firm evidence and showing individuality; engaged with the text/task; paragraphs controlled and linked, sentence length varied, wide vocabulary.
B	Organised with a good understanding of text/task, a good grasp of issues; good range of suitable ideas and evidence; appropriate style engages reader's attention; good vocabulary.
C	Shows a reasonable understanding of text/task; uses evidence to make a range of points; maintains the reader's interest with an appropriate style and suitable vocabulary.
D	Writing not always controlled but a range of vocabulary, and grammar generally accurate. Shows some recognisable sense of argument and persuasion but needs to focus on text/task and prove statements; needs to analyse the story rather than tell it.
E	Shows an understanding of simpler points/issues but needs support and evidence; needs to show engagement with the text/task and attempt balanced argument; shows some evidence of a suitable style but needs to be less repetitive and to improve spelling and grammar.
F	Shows limited understanding of text/task but needs to improve organisation and make statements rather than personal opinions; attempts persuasive argument but needs to widen vocabulary and improve grammatical constructions.
G	Needs to answer in a more meaningful way; and avoid irrelevance and misunderstanding; and improve presentation.

SECTION A: READING

Poetry and How to Revise It

✱ Poetry is examined for both English (1203, 1204) and English Literature (1213).

✱ There are only 16 poems in your Collection: know each of them well.

✱ For English Literature, you'll **definitely** have to compare **2** of them.

✱ For English you'll be looking at **2** of them, and may or may not be asked to make comparisons.

If you work through this guide, doing the exercises and taking advantage of the *Tips for Poetry* on page 72, you will be adequately prepared for both exams.

① Modern Poetry
(English and Literature)

Collection A: In Such a Time as This

Techniques for Revising Poetry: Poem-a-Postcard

This is a very useful form of revision as it enables you to pick out the 'essentials' of a poem and put them on a postcard. Because the postcard is quite small it is a real challenge! You will end up with 16 postcards containing your thoughts on the poems, which you can flick through quickly almost anywhere: even on the way to the exam! Look at the example below.

'Brendon Gallacher' by Jackie Kay	
SUBJECT: A narrative poem telling the story of a girl who has an imaginary friend. She tells her mother all about him as if he was a real person and her mother eventually finds out that there is no such family as the Gallachers. A moment of growing up.	**TONE:** Seemingly naïve, but has an unexpectedly sad ending. **VIEWPOINT:** A child's view of a moment when her imagination is defeated by adult reality. Written in the first person: 'He was seven and I was six'.
USEFUL QUOTES: 'His father was in prison; he was a cat burglar. My father was communist party full-time worker.' 'I'd tell my mum about my Brendon Gallacher.' 'I like meeting him . . . in the open air.' 'She says there are no Gallachers at 24 Novar' 'And he died then . . ./flat out on my bedroom floor . . .'	**USE OF LANGUAGE:** Colloquial: 'A wee holiday', 'his mum'. Repetition of *my* Brendon Gallacher (draws our attention to her 'ownership' of her friend and his very different life). Alliteration: 'funning flapping ear', (emphasises playfulness and listening to each other). Pictorial description through adjectives: 'impish', 'spiky'. No metaphors or similes. Irregular rhyme (verse 1/2 ABCBC). Some half rhymes ('poor/far', 'hair/ear').

1 Use the poem-a-postcard format to do 'Half-past Two' by U.A. Fanthorpe. When you have finished, compare your answers with those on page 74.

2 Use the same headings and work your way through the other 14 poems: perhaps doing one or two a week.

Techniques for Revising Poetry: Diagram Analysis

Any poem can be looked at using this diagram of main pointers:

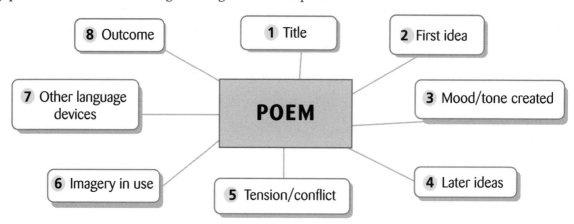

For example: **'The Send-off'** by Wilfred Owen.

1 **What the title suggests:**

People being seen off by other people as they start on a journey. Ironically it would often be a cheerful, exciting occasion but in this instance is not.

2 **First idea:**

Although the men 'sang' as they went to the siding-shed (not the station), the idea of their going somewhere and to something unpleasant is implied through their 'faces grimly gay'.

3 **Mood/tone created:**

The mood is sombre and creates a feeling of unease, 'darkening lanes'; their friends had earlier laden them with 'white' flowers in the form of a 'wreath and spray/As men's [bodies] are, dead'. The mood is finally one of great sadness as many deaths are implied: 'A few . . . creep back'.

4 **Later ideas:**

- Only 'Dull porters' and 'a casual tramp' watch the men leave on the train.

- It is the signal and a lamp which seem more human, as they are personified by a 'nod' and a 'wink'.

- There is a suggestion that the government do not want their activities to be known. They are to go 'secretly, like wrongs hushed-up'.

5 **Tension/conflict:**

There is particular tension in the last verse, which queries if there will be 'wild train-loads' of returning soldiers, but decides that only 'A few . . . may creep back'.

6 **Imagery in use:**

Similes: e.g. 'Their breasts were stuck all white with wreath and spray/As men's are, dead', 'like wrongs hushed-up'.

Personification*: e.g. 'signals nodded', 'a lamp/Winked'.

7 **Other language devices:**

Rhyme scheme: Although the lines are not in regular verse patterns there is a regular rhyme scheme of ABAAB over each set of five lines.

Alliteration*: for emphasis 'grimly gay' (almost contradictory), 'sang . . . siding-shed' (irony), 'so secretly'.

Onomatopoeia: re-enacts the sound: 'beatings of great bells . . . /. . . drums and yells'.

8 **Outcome/final impression(s):**

We are left with a feeling of great sadness that these young men have been sent off to war, and so many will be killed that those who do return will be unable to rejoice. After a long war the roads will be 'half-known', and half-forgotten.

Quick Tip!

* Remember to state the **effect** and **purpose** of personification and alliteration on reader/text in your answer.

1 Now do the same with 'Hide and Seek' by Vernon Scannell.
   When you have finished, compare your answers with those on page 75.

2 Now do the same for the other 14 poems: perhaps doing one or two a week.

1 **What the title suggests:**

5 **Tension/conflict:** (*Is there any?*)

2 **First idea:** (*See lines 1–4*)

6 **Imagery in use:** (*See lines 2 and 19–26*)

3 **Mood/tone created:** (*What does the child feel?*)

7 **Other language devices:** (*Find examples of: alliteration, onomatopoeia, use of verbs, etc. and tell the examiner what they are for*)

4 **Later ideas:**
   i   (*See lines 6–11*)

8 **Outcome/final impression(s):**

   ii   (*See line 13*)

   iii   (*See lines 14–17*)

Quick Tips!

* You will be asked to write about **2 poems**: one of which will be **named**, so you must know **all** the poems in the section you have studied.

* Support your answer by **reference to the text**. Use **brief** quotes. You will not gain marks by quoting more than a few words.

* Bullet points in the question are there to help you answer the question, but **your own response** to the poem is also relevant.

Techniques for Revising Poetry: Comparing Poems, Using Quotes

Your exam questions on poetry require you to compare two or more poems, in terms of the **ideas** and the **language** in which they are expressed. You will need to practise comparing poems. Here is an example:

KEY ELEMENTS	POEM A: 'The Darkling Thrush'		POEM B: 'Electricity Comes to Cocoa Bottom'	
	SIMILARITIES	DIFFERENCES	SIMILARITIES	DIFFERENCES
1 Theme	New beginnings.	The thrush's song heralds the new century and new hope for the world.	New beginnings.	A new life comes to Cocoa Bottom with the advent of electricity.
2 Attitude		Verses 1 and 2 are negative and 'desolate', but verses 3 and 4 are filled with 'joy'.		The attitude is very positive and happy until the last nine lines.
3 Tone/humour/mood	Bleak at first but finally hopeful, expectant of better things.		Happy expectations, but disappointment at end.	
4 Use of imagery, etc.		A poem written long ago: 'nigh', 'sought'. **Form:** A carefully constructed poem with eight syllables to the line and eight lines per verse. **Rhyme:** ABABCDCD. **Metaphor:** 'Frost was spectre-gray'. **Similes:** 'Like strings of broken lyres'. **Personification:** 'The weakening eye of day', 'The Century's corpse outleant', 'His crypt the ... canopy'.		**Form:** Two verses of different lengths with lines of different lengths. **Similes:** 'as soft as chiffon curtains', 'like a pencil line across the sun'. **Personification:** 'a breeze ... held its breath'. **Verbs:** an active poem – verbs used to describe scene: 'swooped', 'gasp', 'fluttering', 'swaying'. **Alliteration:** 'chiffon curtains'. **Repetition:** 'Closing. Closing.'
5 Use of shock tactics		In the bleak evening the thrush in 'full-hearted evensong' changes the atmosphere.		'Is there one among us to record this moment?/But there was none'.
6 Positive ideas		The song of the thrush brings 'blessed Hope' for the new century.		Mr Samuel was 'smiling' and the natural world aflutter at the 'Light! Marvellous light!'
7 Negative ideas	'I was unaware'.	Winter is 'desolate'; frost is a 'spectre'; the short days are 'The weakening eye of the day'.	'It was too late'.	
8 Emotive language (what emotion does the poet create)		The poet is 'fervourless'. The thrush's song brought 'blessed Hope'.		'the moment had passed...' leaves the poem on a sad note.
9 Viewpoint		That of the poet, 'I'.		The narrator who tells the story.

 Now do the same for other pairs of poems, for example 'Where the Scattering Began' and 'Wherever I Hang'.

Collection B: Identity

Techniques for Revising Poetry: Poem-a-Postcard

This is a very useful form of revision as it enables you to pick out the 'essentials' of a poem and put them on a postcard. Because the postcard is quite small it is a real challenge! You will end up with 16 postcards containing your thoughts on the poems, which you can flick through quickly almost anywhere: even on the way to the exam! Look at the example below.

'Warning' by Jenny Joseph	

SUBJECT: Woman with family looks forward to old age. She intends to shock people by her clothes and behaviour so is **warning** them in advance!
Not clear whether she really means it!
	TONE: Humorous. Light-hearted. Positive view of old age.
	
	VIEWPOINT: 1st verse: 'I'
	                         2nd verse: 'You'
	                         3rd verse: 'We'
	                         4th verse: Back to 'I'.

USEFUL QUOTES: 'I shall wear purple/With a red hat' 'gobble up samples in shops' 'make up for the sobriety of my youth' 'learn to spit' 'maybe I ought to practise a little now?'	**USE OF LANGUAGE:** No rhyme. Different line lengths. Lots of nouns (beermats, butter, summer gloves, etc.). Repeats 'I shall' and 'and'. Alliteration: 'satin sandals'. No metaphors/similes.

1 Use the poem-a-postcard format to do 'I Shall Paint My Nails Red' by Carole Satyamurti.
When you have finished, compare your answers with those on page 76.

2 Use the same headings and work your way through the other 14 poems: perhaps doing one or two a week.

Techniques for Revising Poetry: Diagram Analysis

Any poem can be looked at using this diagram of main pointers:

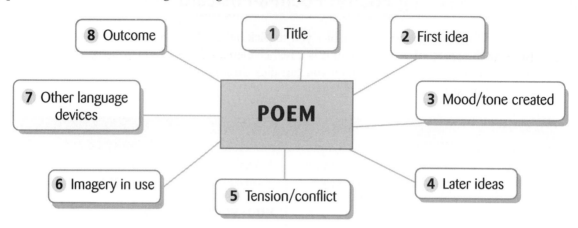

For example: '**Miracle on St. David's Day**' by Gillian Clarke.

1 What the title suggests:

'Miracle' and 'St. David's Day' (1st March) suggest perhaps a religious poem or an unexpected/extraordinary event.

2 First idea:

'It might be a country house'.

3 Mood/tone created:

Mild shock that it is really a mental hospital; great compassion/sympathy for the patients.

4 Later ideas:

- 'I am reading poetry to the insane.'

- 'A big, mild man' who has 'never spoken' suddenly recites "The Daffodils" by Wordsworth.

- The narrator feels 'afraid'; the nurses are 'frozen, alert'.

- Even the flowers seem to be 'still' and listening.

5 Tension/conflict:

The sudden speech of the previously 'dumb' man; the effect it produces on narrator, patients and nurses.

6 Imagery in use:

Many appropriate similes and metaphors, for example,

'The sun treads the path/among cedars'

'In a cage of first March sun'

'like slow/movement of spring water . . . the labourer's voice recites'

'the daffodils are still as wax'.

7 Other language devices:

Alliteration: for emphasis 'He is suddenly standing, silently'.

Shock tactics: 'I am reading poetry to the insane.'

Triple negative: 'a woman/sits **not** listening, **not** seeing, **not feeling**.'

Repetition: 'he rocks'.

8 Outcome/final impression(s):

The dramatic moment of the 'miracle' has passed and peace is restored, even 'before the applause'. The narrator's sympathy for the patients is clear.

1 Now do the same with 'Digging' by Seamus Heaney.
When you have finished, compare your answers with those on page 76.
2 Now do the same for the other 14 poems: perhaps doing one or two a week.

1 **What the title suggests:**

2 **First idea:** (*See lines 1–5*)

3 **Mood/tone created:** (*See lines 15–24*)

4 **Later ideas:**
i   (*See lines 15–16*)

ii (*See lines 17–24*)

iii (*See line 28*)

iv (*See lines 29–31*)

5 **Tension/conflict:** (*Is there any?*)

6 **Imagery in use:** (*See line 2*)

7 **Other language devices:** (*Find examples of: alliteration, onomatopoeia, use of verbs etc. and tell the examiner what they are for*)

8 **Outcome/final impression(s):**

Techniques for Revising Poetry: Comparing Poems, Using Quotes

Your exam questions on poetry require you to compare two or more poems, in terms of the **ideas** and the **language** in which they are expressed. You will need to practise comparing poems. Here is an example:

KEY ELEMENTS	POEM A: 'Mirror'		POEM B: 'Warning'	
	SIMILARITIES	DIFFERENCES	SIMILARITIES	DIFFERENCES
1 Theme	Old age.		Old age.	
2 Attitude		Negative, fearful.		Positive, humorous.
3 Tone/humour/mood		Serious; not funny but some irony (e.g. 'a little god, four-cornered').		Contrasts present with would-be outrageous future (see verse 1).
4 Use of imagery, etc.	Colour (silver, pink).	Water (verse 2). (Extended metaphor) 'lake', 'reflect', 'drowned', 'fish'.	Colour (red and purple).	No metaphors/similes. Mundane objects (nouns) contrasted 'satin sandals … butter'. Repeats 'and' and 'I shall'.
5 Use of shock tactics		'like a terrible fish'.		'press alarm bells' 'learn to spit'.
6 Positive ideas		Youth is preferable to old age; truth to lies.		The future might be freer, more exciting.
7 Negative ideas		Old age is frightening/upsetting.		'Now' is too boring/respectable.
8 Emotive language (what emotion does the poet create)		Fear (of the future) 'tears'; anxiety ('agitation of hands').		Hope; admiration of rebelliousness.
9 Viewpoint	Feminine.	The 'Mirror' itself is the narrator.	Feminine.	The poet herself seems to be the first person narrator.

Now do the same for other pairs of poems, for example 'Once Upon a Time' and 'Follower'.

Collection C: Nature

Techniques for Revising Poetry: Poem-a-Postcard

This is a very useful form of revision as it enables you to pick out the 'essentials' of a poem and put them on a postcard. Because the postcard is quite small it is a real challenge! You will end up with 16 postcards containing your thoughts on the poems, which you can flick through almost anywhere: even on the way to the exam!

Look at the example below.

'A Blade of Grass' by Brian Patten	
SUBJECT: Poet asked for poem – by a girlfriend, perhaps. He offers instead a blade of grass, in order to point out the superiority of nature to man-made products. The grass is the poem's central symbol, standing for one small token of nature, found everywhere, but each blade uniquely precious.	**TONE:** Light-hearted but thought-provoking (i.e. not entirely serious even though making a serious point). **VIEWPOINT:** The 'I' of the poet, the 'you' of the female listener. They have contrasting viewpoints.
USEFUL QUOTES: 'It is more immediate/ Than any image of my making.' 'Anyone can offer a blade of grass.' 'as you grow older/A blade of grass/Becomes more difficult to accept.'	**USE OF LANGUAGE:** no rhyme; different line lengths; simple diction. Absence of metaphorical language but a central symbol of the blade of grass. Repetition of 'a blade of grass'.

1 Use the poem-a-postcard format to do 'The Thought-Fox' by Ted Hughes. When you have finished, compare your answers with those on page 77.
2 Use the same headings and work your way through the other 14 poems: perhaps doing one or two a week.

Techniques for Revising Poetry: Diagram Analysis

Any poem can be looked at using this diagram of main pointers:

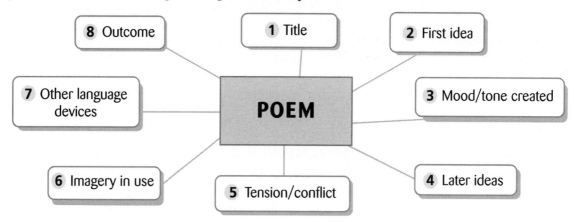

For example: '**Break of Day in the Trenches**' by Isaac Rosenberg.

1   What the title suggests:

'Trenches' suggests warfare, specifically World War One.

2   First idea:

As dawn breaks a rat startles the poet.

3   Mood/tone created:

The breaking of the day here is not conventionally a time of renewed hope – but brings with it a sense of despair.

4   Later ideas:

The poet is fascinated by the rat's sense of superiority:

- It is 'queer sardonic', 'droll', 'cosmopolitan'.
- It grins 'inwardly' at the young soldiers.
- It senses that it has more chance of survival than them.

5   Tension/conflict:

The conflict arises from the turning over of the usual stereotypes – that man is vastly superior to the scavenging rat. In this case it is the soldier who is condemned to live in a filthy trench, with a short life-expectancy, whilst the rat can move freely.

6   Imagery in use:

Powerful metaphorical language e.g.

- 'the same old druid Time'
- 'Bonds to the whims of murder'
- 'Sprawled in the bowels of the earth'
- 'The torn fields of France'
- 'the shrieking iron and flame'
- 'Poppies whose roots are in man's veins'.

7   Other language devices:

Powerful use of symbols: the poppy, the rat, the dust, the sleeping green.

8   Outcome/final impression(s):

The poet clearly senses the likelihood of his own death but is philosophical about it. The carnage and sheer horror soon to start up again contrasts with the peaceful moment's reflection brought about by the rat.

Quick Tip!

* Remember always to explain what effect a figure of speech achieves and what the poet is aiming for.

1 Now do the same with 'Keeping Orchids' by Jackie Kay.
When you have finished, compare your answers with those on page 77.

2 Now do the same for the other 14 poems: perhaps doing one or two a week.

1 **What the title suggests:** *(What do orchids connote and how can you 'keep' them alive or any other flower?)*

5 **Tension/conflict:** *(Where might there be tension and conflict if an adopted person met their birth-mother?)*

2 **First idea:** *(See lines 1–3)*

6 **Imagery in use:** *(Find strong and effective metaphors and similes e.g. in lines 3, 4, 11, 13, 14. Note also the poet's tremendous use of symbolism e.g. the orchids, the glass carafe, and Time)*

3 **Mood/tone created:** *(See lines 6–7)*

7 **Other language devices:** *(Look in particular for examples of alliteration)*

4 **Later ideas:**
i *(See lines 10–11)*

ii *(See lines 13–14)*

iii *(See lines 17–19)*

iv *(See lines 23–24)*

v *(See lines 25–29)*

8 **Outcome/final impression(s):** *(What does the poet feel at the end about her mother and her own life from now on?)*

Techniques for Revising Poetry: Comparing Poems, Using Quotes

Your exam questions on poetry require you to compare two or more poems, in terms of the **ideas** and the **language** in which they are expressed. You will need to practise comparing poems. Here is an example:

KEY ELEMENTS	POEM A: 'Nettles' SIMILARITIES	POEM A: 'Nettles' DIFFERENCES	POEM B: 'Thistles' SIMILARITIES	POEM B: 'Thistles' DIFFERENCES
1 Theme	i Man is vulnerable to pain inflicted by nature's barbs. ii When man attempts to remove the source of danger nature patiently renews itself.	The nettles are only attacked by the poet after his son's chance encounter with them.	i Man suffers when coming into conflict with nature's element. ii When under attack the thistle fights back more strongly than before.	Beast and man are in permanent natural conflict with the thistles.
2 Attitude	Resilience of nature.	Man must learn to accept natural pain which is a fact of life.	Strength and combative aspects of nature.	Thistles are no better (or worse) than Man in their warlike activities.
3 Tone/humour/mood	Serious comment on natural conflict.	Human nature and suffering provide a sombre tone, a passive mood at the end.	Serious comment on natural conflict.	Human nature only briefly touched on; thistles are responsible for the defiant, belligerent tone.
4 Use of imagery, etc.	'green spears', 'regiment of spite', 'fierce parade'. Martial images.	'A funeral pyre to burn the fallen dead'.	'spike the summer air', 'splintered weapons', 'Stiff with weapons'. Martial images.	Extended metaphor of plant of Scandinavian qualities (and origins).
5 Use of shock tactics	The extended metaphor of war and weaponry.	The pain inflicted on the boy: 'White blisters beaded on his tender skin'.	The extended metaphor of weapons and feuding.	The feuding nature of the plant; 'Every one a revengeful burst Of resurrection'. To some extent they derive from our war-like (Viking) ancestors.
6 Positive ideas	Nature cannot be restrained or eliminated.	Man can learn from nature and its painful lessons.	Nature will strike back if threatened.	Man and nature have fighting qualities in common.
7 Negative ideas	It's impossible for humans to get on top of troublesome weeds. Trying to get rid of them is a wasteful, painful effort.	Life is full of painful experiences.	Any attempt to get rid of the thistles will fail spectacularly.	Man is doomed to grow 'grey' and die; he fights and kills his own kind, repeatedly, down the generations.
8 Emotive language (what emotion does the poet create)	'slashed in fury' (anger).	'With sobs and tears/The boy came seeking comfort'; 'tender skin' (pathos/sympathy); 'My son would often feel sharp wounds again' (resignation).	'crackle open' 'a grasping fistful' etc. (anger).	'fighting back over the same old ground' (despair).
9 Viewpoint	Nature is spiteful, as can be mankind.	Personal: the poet is actively and emotionally involved as a result of his son's pain.	Nature is spiteful and so is mankind.	Written in third person: poet takes an overview without real emotional involvement or bias.

Now do the same for other pairs of poems, for example 'Wind' and 'The Storm'.

② Non-fiction Prose
English A (1203) Paper 2F or 4H

The Literary Non-fiction Texts

Viewpoint and Tone

In this section we are looking at autobiography and travel writing.

* Their aim is to educate.

* They have an underlying seriousness of purpose.

* The author writes from real experience and with an overview.

* His or her tone of 'voice' is personal.

Fill in a chart similar to the one below, using examples from the text you are studying. An example has been done for you.

> **TEXT: 'Mongolian wedding' from *In the Empire of Genghis Khan* by Stanley Stewart**
>
> **REAL EXPERIENCE**
> The author, a guest at a Mongolian wedding, witnesses the proceedings: the two families present in large numbers, the excessive hospitality, the uproar and blows being exchanged.
>
> **AMUSING/ENTERTAINING ASPECT**
> The punch-up is the most amusing incident, with both the bride and the groom's friends and families exchanging blows whilst the bridal couple sit passively, and the priest helps himself to a sly drink. After honour has been satisfied, the drinking and singing resumes.
>
> **SERIOUS UNDERLYING PURPOSE**
> Stanley Stewart is making serious points about Mongolian culture. A wedding is not only a time for feasting and celebration but for one side of the family to try to establish superiority over the other. It is, apparently, fairly typical for the occasion to 'degenerate into a brawl'. The whole affair is 'a mixture of camaraderie and violence'.
>
> **VIEWPOINT**
> The author, a travel writer in pursuit of interesting cultural insights, takes a wryly amused overview of the wedding, at which he is a guest. He observes, records, exaggerates no doubt, but does not judge.
>
> **TONE**
> Light, sarcastic, ironic. The reader takes very little at face-value. The tone is established, in this extract, by the guest warning the writer about other people's boisterous behaviour and admitting to being as bad himself.

Quick Tip!

* Depth of interest and tension can be introduced by sharing different viewpoints.

How seriously are we supposed to take Stanley Stewart's depiction of a Mongolian wedding? Do we find any aspects shocking or unbelievable? Support your answer with close reference to the text. Spend 40 minutes on this.

Characters

Characters in this type of writing tend not to be as developed as in works of fiction. It is, however, necessary to understand them.

Fill in a chart similar to the one below, using examples from the text you are studying. An example has been done for you.

TEXT: *The Other Side of the Dale* by Gervase Phinn   **Character:** Joseph Barclay

PHYSICAL DESCRIPTION
'a small serious-faced boy with thick-lensed glasses'; old-fashioned short-back-and-sides hairstyle; 'could have been a schoolboy of the 1950s'.

BACKGROUND
Eleven years old; the author of an account of the school's history; a 'precocious pupil'.

PERSONALITY
Old-fashioned, highly intelligent; very well-ordered; serious-minded.

IS THE CHARACTER TRUE TO LIFE OR EXAGGERATED?
The author gives no indication, by tone or manner, that the characters are exaggerated. Joseph does not appear as a caricature but simply as an unusually old-fashioned and precocious boy.

Quick Tip!

* First impressions, the writer's or your own, are very important when judging character in this type of writing.

 How are people and relationships portrayed in the text you are studying? Spend 40 minutes on this.

Language and Style: Atmosphere and Mood

Look at the way the author varies sentence length and uses distinctive words and phrases to capture **atmosphere** and **mood**. An example has been done for you.

TEXT: 'Don't leave me here to die' by Cathy O'Dowd

SHORT SENTENCES – to create excitement/tension

Note the cluster of short sentences when Cathy O'Dowd kneels down next to the injured climber. The three-word utterance 'I felt sick' speaks volumes about what she is experiencing, but does not slow down the narrative. Note, too, the penultimate paragraph which records the decision to leave Fran on the mountain.

LONG SENTENCES – to suggest peace/contemplation

The fourth paragraph has long sentences, to capture the deep thoughts that are flooding through the minds of members of the climbing party as they contemplate what to do with 'the body'.

POETIC OR FIGURATIVE LANGUAGE (e.g. metaphors and similes) – to suggest feeling

Fran is described as 'like a porcelain doll', 'as helpless as a rag doll', and having legs 'as useless as strands of spaghetti', figurative images which suggest a lack of strength and coordination.

DIALOGUE – to create character or involve the reader

The brief dialogue between Cathy and Fran dramatises a scene where words are in short supply. Cathy is lost in thought about what to do; Fran is desperate and incoherent ('"Why are you doing this to me?" she asked').

Quick Tip!

✱ Mood and atmosphere can be achieved by the use of precise and vivid detail.

Use all of the above information to write about how effectively the writer uses language and style to create atmosphere and mood. Spend 40 minutes on this.

Structure, Presentation and Layout

Structure is the way a text has been put together. Here are some questions that will help you to analyse structure, presentation and layout, and some model answers.

HOW DOES THE TEXT LOOK ON THE PAGE?
Describe the layout of 'Don't leave me here to die'.
This extract was published in *The Guardian* and has a broadsheet's format of headline and columns. It has the appearance of a feature article.

HOW ARE THE IDEAS/EVENTS DEVELOPED FROM ONE PARAGRAPH TO ANOTHER?
Consider this with regard to *In the Empire of Genghis Khan*.
Several of the early paragraphs begin by referring to time or waiting for an event to happen. Later paragraphs are used to introduce new characters and sequence events.

DOES THE TEXT HAVE A LINEAR FORM?
Consider the extract from *The Other Side of the Dale*, and say whether events unfold as they happen.
Written in linear form i.e. the events unfold in order of time, beginning with the arrival of the narrator/school inspector and moving through the morning's events. However, the device of the school logbooks is used to give some historical perspective.

DOES THE TEXT INCORPORATE OTHER FORMS?
Consider the effect achieved by the brief passage in playscript form in 'The Lady in the Van' from *Writing Home*.
The story is told in a sort of diary form, with events tied to time. The small passage of playscript allows Miss Shepherd's meeting with her social worker to be in a more dramatic form. We actually witness the events rather than having them reported.

Quick Tip!

✳ Paragraph length controls the sequence and speed of events.

Work through all the texts using a chart like the one above to plot structure, presentation and layout.

The Media Non-fiction Texts

Anchoring

In this section we are looking at newspaper articles. Use the following questions to 'anchor' each text.

1 What type of writing is it and who wrote it?

....

....

2 Who is the intended audience?

....

....

3 What is the writer's viewpoint?

....

....

4 How does the writer want the audience to respond?

....

....

5 How does the writer persuade us to agree?

....

....

6 What is the writer's tone?

....

....

Quick Tip!

✱ A fact is something that is true; an opinion is what a person feels about something.

Consider the introductions to two or three of the newspaper articles and say how effective they are as 'hooks' to attract the reader's attention. Spend 40 minutes on this.

Arguments and Issues

Summarise the views for and against the issues raised. Some of the boxes have been completed for you, as examples.

ISSUE: School Sport		
Author	**FOR**	**AGAINST**
Harris		Many pupils are intimidated by having to do Games and the aggressive attitude of some PE teachers.
Borger		
Berliner		
McNeil	Being actively involved with sport improves health and has personal and social benefits.	

ISSUE: Corporal Punishment		
Author	**FOR**	**AGAINST**
Frean	Complete avoidance of physical restraint has led to children being uncontrollable.	
Norton		
Bunting		There are far more effective ways of controlling children: it is better to persuade by example than to enforce by punishment.
Bailie and others		

Quick Tip!

* Remember a journalist may put across both sides of an argument – but encourage the reader to one side rather than the other.

Consider the way two authors put across opposing arguments about either sport or parenting. Spend 40 minutes on this.

Language and Style

Complete a chart like the one below for all of the articles that you are revising.

TITLE:
USE OF RESEARCH OR SURVEYS
FACTS AND STATISTICS
JARGON/SPECIALISED VOCABULARY
USE OF EXPERT OPINION
EMOTIVE LANGUAGE/IMAGES
CAN YOU SPOT ANY BIAS? HOW STRONG IS IT?

An example has been done for you on page 78.

Quick Tip!

✱ Most of these passages show a variation of language styles.

Write a report on school sport, summarising the arguments in Wendy Berliner's article. Spend 40 minutes on this.

Presentation and Layout

Consider the use made of the following:

HEADLINE – is it informative? any puns or wordplay?

COLUMNS AND FONT STYLE

QUOTATIONS

VARIATION OF SENTENCE AND PARAGRAPH LENGTH

Quick Tips!

✱ Broadsheet newspapers tend to use formal language and give a reasonably balanced treatment of serious issues.

✱ You will not be expected to say too much about the layout of these passages because they are from broadsheets not tabloids.

Newspaper articles are often constructed in three parts: the **introduction**, the **elaboration**, which develops the ideas introduced and the **projection**, which looks forward to future developments. Consider how one or two of the articles conform to this format. Spend 40 minutes on this.

The Unseen Passage

Students doing GCSE English Specification B (1204) 3F or 5H do one question on an unprepared non-fiction text. If you work through this entire revision guide you will be adequately prepared to tackle any of the various possible genres, for example autobiography or discursive articles, on which you might be examined.

Higher tier

Here is an example of an unseen discursive text, abbreviated from one which appeared in the quality Sunday broadsheet, *The Observer*. Read it and then answer the question at the end.

Should it be a crime to hit your child?

Now that childminders face a ban on striking their charges, some argue that even parents should lose the right to smack.

A child is screaming in the aisle of a super-market. He is four years old. His mother, laden with groceries at the end of a long day at work, is struggling to get to the check-out before the shop closes. She has tried reason. She has used all the 'positive alternatives' recommended in self-help books. She doesn't want to give the boy the chocolate he is demanding. . .

The boy carries on screaming, louder and louder. He is throwing food around. As his mother starts to queue, the boy makes a bolt for the door and out into the busy street. His mother dashes out and grabs him just before he steps into the road. 'Don't you ever do that again,' she shouts, delivering a smack, sharp and stinging, across the back of the legs. The child whimpers. And finally stops crying.

Similar scenes take place every day across the country, and we all react in different ways. Whether a father of three or a single woman with no children enjoying a drink in the pub, everyone has an opinion on smacking and, by extension, corporal punishment. This week the Government will gingerly enter one of the most sensitive national debates: who has the right to strike a child? And who has the right to tell parents who that person should be?

By autumn the Government plans to make smacking illegal for tens of thousands of childminders across England ... At present, with the agreement of the parents, childminders can smack children within the bounds of 'reasonable chastisement' under the 140-year-old law which still governs parents' physical relationship with their children. Changing that law is one of the strongest signals the Government can give that it does not approve of smacking, beyond banning it totally. And it is a significant U-turn.

. . .

Since Sweden banned smacking a decade ago child deaths at the hands of parents have fallen to zero. In Britain it is running at one a week. Countless studies say that smacking does not work, it merely gives children the sense that violence is an appropriate response to get what you want. Smacking could also leave psychological as well as physical scars.

. . .

Now childcare organisations are asking: why not go the whole way, bringing the UK into line with UN demands and banning smacking outright? 'This is another step towards getting the public to accept that children should not be smacked,' said one senior NSPCC official.

Kamal Ahmed
Sunday May 4, 2003
The Observer

Discuss in detail the issues raised by Kamal Ahmed and say how effective you find the article. You should refer, among other things, to:
 ✳ the writer's use of detail and techniques of persuasion
 ✳ the language and structure of the passage
 ✳ appropriate evidence to support your points.
Spend 40 minutes on this.

Foundation tier

Read the passage adapted from an article which appeared in the *Positive Parenting Newsletter*. What does the author, Deborah Critzer-Fox, an American 'Parenting Educator', have to say of value on how parents can best communicate with their children?

You should write about, amongst other things:

* the advice she gives to parents
* her attitude to parenting
* the misunderstandings that can occur between parents and their children.

Support your answer with examples from the text. Spend 40 minutes on this.

Effective discipline has much more to do with communication than control. Many parents feel that to control their children is to be a good parent. However, studies have shown that less coercive discipline can be related to better outcomes for children. If the coercive parenting is replaced with a firm and kind style, communication that relates to the child at his or her level, and discipline that builds the child's self-esteem, then the child will tend to do better. True parental power is being able to influence the child to behave better, while building self-esteem, and teaching long-range life skills. Here are five of the best communication ideas that will contribute to creating this result:

1. Write to your child. Beginning at a very young age, parents can incorporate written communication into the parenting style. This idea can begin young, as early as three or four. At this time, since the child cannot yet read, the parent should write in pictures, a happy face to say 'Good for you!' or a cartoon, on their bedroom door, of parents sleeping to remind kids not to wake parents early on Saturdays. When the child is of school age, the notes can be placed in lunch boxes, or handed to kids on their way to school. Parents that write notes report that children also begin to use this method of communication. Wouldn't it be nice to receive a request or complaint in writing so you have time to think over your response?

2. Think it over. Give your child's ideas and opinions a great deal of credence. Whenever possible, verbalise your thought processes in thinking over a particular situation. When your child understands that you are giving weight and consideration to his or her concern, you are more likely to have a better outcome if you need to deny the request. Look at the situation from the child's perspective with understanding and detail.

3. Lead the child to the answer. Often, the parent knows the best answer to any given situation. But it is often of little value to tell the child the 'answer'. The most effective and beneficial way of handling these situations is through leading the child to come up with the answer him or her self. Help the child work through the pros and cons of an issue, while maintaining a neutral stance. The child begins to trust that you have faith in his or her ability to work out problems and will begin to ask your opinion and advice. When a parent *always* tells the child what to do, the child will see them as an adversary. There are times when you need to 'tell it like it is', but there are far more opportunities to take this other approach as well.

4. Maintain integrity. Parents are notorious for bending and breaking the truth with children! If you believe in truthfulness, do not lie to your kids, ask them to lie for you or make excuses for lying. We begin this 'fuzziness' with the truth with our children at a very young age. Before they are able to tell the time, we put them off with 'Just a minute' or 'Later' but this can undermine children's respect for us as parents over time. Kids will begin to beg, plead and pester. It is better to be as honest and clear as possible – tell them *exactly* when you will respond, *exactly* how much time and *follow through* to the minute!

5. Maintain physical closeness and connection. Many parents are afraid to be physically close to their children. However, *children and all of us* need physical closeness! Hugging, cuddling, playful fighting, rocking, stroking hair, massages and bear hugs are just a few ways to be physical with kids. When you speak to a child, how about placing a gentle hand on their shoulder? Maintaining this physical connection takes work, particularly as children become teens and may go through stages of resisting touch. Usually they are testing their boundaries, so be respectful.

Discipline does not need to be punitive, coercive, manipulative or negative. Children can learn in a positive, upbeat, firm and kind environment much better than in a negative one. Parents set the tone for the family environment and so have great influence over the nature of it. I believe that we parents have so much more influence in our families than we realize. We need to take this influence to heart, strive to do our very best and never give up on our kids!

Deborah Critzer-Fox
Positive Parenting Newsletter
www.positiveparenting.com

Different Cultures and Traditions

English Specification B (1204)
Paper 2F or 4H

Themes, Conflict and Moral Attitudes

Themes: These are the underlying or unifying ideas that appear throughout a text. They reflect aspects of the main subject and the author's purpose. 'The Gold Cadillac' by Mildred Taylor has been used as an example in the box below.

Key theme: Racial discrimination
SECONDARY THEMES
• Growing up/rites of passage.
• Prejudice in its many forms.
• Family strength and stability.
• Possessions and false values.

Conflict: This is the struggle or contest, often more mental than physical, that occurs in all short stories, providing the central issue, often the mainspring of the plot.

In **'The Gold Cadillac'** by Mildred Taylor there are two areas of conflict, one within the family and one within society.

CAUSE OF CONFLICT	WHO IS INVOLVED IN IT?
Could the family afford such an expensive car when saving for a house?	Mother and father.
Right of the family to drive the car in Mississippi.	Black family and white society.

Moral Attitudes: These are what govern the beliefs and behaviour of people. Different people, of course, may have different views of right and wrong. The **author's** moral attitude is often implied rather than stated and can generally be supported by reason. The **central character's** view is often similar to the author's but not always.

Look for the following and supply evidence:

MORAL ATTITUDE OF A MAJOR CHARACTER
'lois, young and innocent, has no concept of racial prejudice before meeting it in the Deep South. She can't understand, for example, why her mother does not want to go to Mississippi, the significance of the 'Whites Only' signs in Tennessee, or why her father is bullied by the policemen.
FIND A DIFFERENT CHARACTER WHO SHOWS A DIFFERENT MORAL STANDPOINT
The white policemen condemn the black people on sight. They address the father disrespectfully as 'boy', call him a liar when he claims ownership of the car, and search him. They detain him for more than three hours and trump up a speeding charge. After that they 'drive' him out of town. Quite clearly they are racially motivated – and cannot believe such people could own such a car.
THE MORAL ATTITUDE OF THE AUTHOR
The author's attitude is not stated directly because she tells her story through the eyes of 'lois. But we assume from her choice of characters, story and setting that she is writing to expose and condemn the racism of the period.

Now complete the table below for another short story.

TITLE:
Key Theme:

SECONDARY THEMES

-
-
-
-

CAUSE OF CONFLICT	WHO IS INVOLVED IN IT?

MORAL ATTITUDE OF A MAJOR CHARACTER

FIND A DIFFERENT CHARACTER WHO SHOWS A DIFFERENT MORAL STANDPOINT

THE MORAL ATTITUDE OF THE AUTHOR

 If you have done 'A Stench of Kerosene' by Amrita Pritam, compare your answers with those on page 78.

Quick Tip!

✱ When writing about themes, conflicts or moral attitudes, some will obviously require more emphasis than others.

Characters

Short stories:

* have a limited number of characters (sometimes only one)

* are not described in detail

* do not have too much depth.

Often we judge characters best through their actions, particularly if put in context by taking into account:

* their exterior detail i.e. appearance, personal history, social position etc.

* their significant thoughts and statements.

The chart below shows you how to do this.

TITLE: 'The Schoolteacher's Guest' by Isabel Allende

Main Character: Ines, the schoolteacher

DETAILS OF APPEARANCE/POSITION ETC.
Retired village schoolteacher; now owner of boarding house; son murdered; 'the most respected matron in all Agua Santa'; 'counsellor, arbiter, and judge in all the town's problems'.

ROLE IN STORY
Central character, at the heart of the story. Her action, in avenging her son's death, provides interest/impetus.

CHARACTER THROUGH ACTION

ACTION	WHAT IT TELLS US
i Takes charge of boarding house after retiring from teaching.	Active personality; doesn't want to be idle; needs stimulation to avoid boredom.
ii Went into village jail, freed one of her students accused of drunkenness and gave him a smack.	Determined, forceful, no-nonsense personality, with commonsense approach to justice and lack of faith in legal system.
iii Kills her son's 'murderer' with a machete.	Though she takes revenge as her right and duty, she does it as efficiently and as painlessly as possible, showing a kind of compassion for her victim.
iv Scrubs the walls and furniture in the dead man's room, burns the bed clothes and airs the house.	Brisk and efficient; wants to be rid of the evidence and to resume her life.

SIGNIFICANT THOUGHTS OR STATEMENTS
'I came up behind him and lopped off his head with one swing. He never knew what hit him, poor man.' (Lines 98–99).

'I had to do it, it was fate.' (Line 101).

'I've been waiting all these years; I knew he would come sooner or later.' (Line 105).

SUMMARY OF PERSONALITY AND MOTIVATION
Ines is a strong-minded, independent sort, briskly efficient and purposeful in all things and highly respected by the town's people. After her son's death, she is silently motivated by desire for revenge. She waits patiently for the opportunity, convinced fate will bring it her way. When it arises she takes it without hesitation. Even though she has no remorse for what she has done, nevertheless she has a kind of sympathy for the dead man. She is a complex character, then, in many ways superior to her environment, even though sharing the local belief in the individual's right to retribution.

Now complete the table below for the secondary character, Riad Halabi.

Secondary Character: Riad Halabi

DETAILS OF APPEARANCE/POSITION ETC.

ROLE IN STORY

CHARACTER THROUGH ACTION

ACTION	WHAT IT TELLS US
i	
ii	
iii	

SIGNIFICANT THOUGHTS OR STATEMENTS

SUMMARY OF PERSONALITY AND MOTIVATION

Quick Tip!

* It is very useful to do character charts in this way for all the short stories – if time allows.

 When you have finished, compare your answers with those on page 79.

Plot

Although the plot of a short story tends to be simple and involve only one outcome, its structure is like other forms of fiction. The following chart is very useful for schematising the plot.

1 Complete the chart for 'Country Lovers', by Nadine Gordimer, expanding on the headings provided, and finding key supporting quotations.

2 After completing the chart, write about the importance of the plot to Njabulo, Thebedi's husband. Spend 40 minutes on this.

3 Then use this plot chart to record details of the other stories.

OPENING SITUATION: Children at play on the farm: Paulus and Thebedi

Key quotes:

FIRST MAJOR EVENT: Paulus and Thebedi form relationship

Key quotes:

COMPLICATION: Thebedi has a baby

Key quotes:

CRISIS POINT: Death of baby

Key quotes:

TENSION OR SUSPENSE: Courtroom scene

Key quotes:

HOW IT ALL ENDS: Court's verdict, situation of characters

Key quotes:

Quick Tip!

✱ One of the best ways of discovering how much progress a plot achieves is by comparing circumstances at the beginning of the story with those at the end.

Culture, Tradition, Atmosphere and Setting

All of the stories in the collection have a strong cultural background. When reading them remember these formulas:

$$Setting = Place + Period$$

$$Culture = Setting + People$$

1 For each of the short stories complete the chart. The first one has been done for you. The answer for the rest appears on page 79, to compare when you have finished.

Title	Place and period	Cultural issues
'Country Lovers'	South African farm and village.	Apartheid; illegality of mixed marriages.

2 For as many of the stories as possible, complete the following table using examples and quotations. 'Vendetta' has been done for you. Remember that **atmosphere** is the mood of a place. It may change, depending on how people respond at different times.

TITLE: 'Vendetta' by Guy de Maupassant	
Questions	Examples and quotations
How is the scene set and what is its atmosphere?	A bleak, desolate island setting. The widow's 'mean house' is on 'the ramparts' of Bonifacio, which, itself, is 'built on a spur of the mountain and in places actually overhanging the sea'. The sea and coast 'are forever harassed by a restless wind'. Atmosphere is tempestuous/threatening/depressing.
How do the characters respond to their background?	After the death of her son, the widow 'sat alone at her window gazing at the opposite coast and thinking of her revenge'. It is as if her hatred is in tune with the landscape and gains strength from it.
Where in the story does the atmosphere change?	At the point where the widow has an 'inspiration of savage, vindictive ferocity'. She now has a sense of purpose, and we hear no more of the bleak and depressing background.
How big a part does culture and tradition play in the story?	It is clear that in Corsica there was an obligation to avenge the murder of a relative. The widow's problem is that her son 'had no brother, nor any near male relation. There was no man in the family who could take up the vendetta'. It is for this reason she has to devise her own plan.
What is the atmosphere at the end of the story and how has it changed from the beginning?	When the widow has trained Sémillante to her satisfaction and is on the point of taking her revenge, her mood is entirely different from her earlier brooding lethargy; she goes to confession 'in an ecstasy of devotion', and then is purposeful about her business, disguising herself and sailing to Sardinia. When she returns, her job done, 'she slept well'. The story ends calmly.

Quick Tip!

* To see how important culture is, try transporting one story's background to another's – and note the effect.

Key Quotes and Speeches

 Copy this table and fill it in for each of the short stories.

TITLE:			
Characters	**Themes**	**Atmosphere**	**Setting**
MAIN	MAIN	BEGINNING	HISTORICAL/ CULTURAL
SECONDARY	SECONDARY	MIDDLE	GEOGRAPHICAL
		END	LOCATIONS

FIND A QUOTATION WHICH SEEMS TO MOST SUM UP THE STORY

FIND A QUOTATION WHICH SEEMS TO MOST SUM UP THE CULTURAL ISSUE OF THE STORY

Comparing Stories

Remember you will be answering on two stories. Completing this chart will help you to compare them.

STORIES	'Country Lovers'	'Veronica'
Characters	Thebedi	Veronica
SIMILARITIES		
DIFFERENCES		

STORIES	'Veronica'	'A Stench of Kerosene'
Setting	A Nigerian village	A Northern Indian village
SIMILARITIES		
DIFFERENCES		

STORIES	'The Gold Cadillac'	'Country Lovers'
Theme	Racism	
SIMILARITIES		
DIFFERENCES		

STORIES	'Vendetta'	'The Schoolteacher's Guest'
Cultural issue	Blood revenge/the 'law of retaliation'	
SIMILARITIES		
DIFFERENCES		

 When you have finished, compare your answers with those on page 80.

Quick Tip!

* When revising for the exam be aware that all the stories have one theme in common. What is it? Turn to page 80 to find out.

4 Media

In the exam (English Specification A) you will be asked to read an unseen piece of media, probably:

✽ a newspaper extract or

✽ a magazine article or

✽ a leaflet or

✽ a broadcast item, e.g. a scripted interview.

✽ You will have 40 minutes to answer the question.

✽ Reading it over carefully several times is essential.

✽ Feel free to highlight or underline where you need to. This will help you to find things more easily later.

The question may focus on:

✽ the use of PHOTOGRAPHS and ILLUSTRATIONS

✽ the use of HEADLINES and CAPTIONS

✽ the CONTENT of the piece

✽ the writer's USE OF LANGUAGE

✽ any other features of LAYOUT and DESIGN.

Techniques for Revising Media: The 5 'Ws'

whowhatwhenwherewhy

Who is supporting the Teenage Cancer Trust's annual bandanna auction? Fashion stars including John Galliano, Dolce & Gabbana and Marni have designed bandannas to be auctioned in September in aid of the charity. Inquiries: www.teencancer.org

When should trainer fanatics look out for Puma's Shudoh Tang limited edition sneakers? They will go on sale on September 19, and only 888 pairs will be sold at Puma stores and at Shanghai Tang – the boutique that collaborated on the design.

What will be the biggest hit at Miss Selfridge this autumn? The "Originals" collection, based on pictures from the company's archives. Now in stores in Leeds, Liverpool, Edinburgh, Belfast, Birmingham and at Oxford Circus, the range coincides with this autumn's biggest trend – the Sixties look – and includes checked wool jackets, knitwear and mini shift dresses.

Where can you get a cut-price haircut and give to charity at the same time? Charles Worthington-trained Karine Jackson is launching her Covent Garden salon at 24 Litchfield Street on August 21, with a day of discounted appointments. The proceeds from cuts, manicures and pedicures will go directly to Hope and Homes for Children.

Why is Australian Bodycare's Tea Tree Oil a must-have for your holiday beauty bag? The potion can be used to cure bites, stings, cuts and burns, as well as being a powerful antiseptic. The 7.5ml bottle costs £3.99 and is available from chemists nationwide.

Clare Coulson
The Daily Telegraph
11th August 2003

Newspaper articles use the 5 'Ws' to make sure the reader finds out the important facts. Read Clare Coulson's article. It gives details of the 5 'Ws' she thinks desirable or of interest.

Complete the chart below listing the 5 'Ws' **you** consider most desirable. Write a brief paragraph on each, setting it out in the same manner as the article.

Who	Where
When	
	Why
What	

Quick Tip!

* If you are asked to write a newspaper article in the Writing Triplets don't forget to use the 5 'Ws' in the first and second paragraphs.

Newspapers

In the examination you are asked to look at the way in which an article is structured to achieve the most **impact** on the reader. You will analyse how the photographs, headlines, the content of the article and the language used, work together to give the facts and possibly to influence the reader through the use of opinions.

1829 George Stephenson's Rocket, 30mph

1934 Flying Scotsman, first passenger train to reach 100mph

1938 Mallard, 126mph, remains fastest speed for steam locomotive

2003 Eurostar, 208mph

208mph: In the tracks of Rocket and Mallard, Eurostar breaks British record

The age of the high-speed train roared into Britain yesterday when a Eurostar train shattered the 200mph barrier. Powering slightly downhill through the north Kent countryside, Train 3134 reached 208mph (334.7kph) while pulling 14 cars.

About 80 rail managers and engineers on board broke into applause as the speed was verified, easily eclipsing the previous domestic record of 162mph by a subsequently abandoned British Rail tilt train prototype in 1979.

However, the French were not particularly impressed. Their locomotive named Bo Bo passed the 200mph mark in 1955.

A more sophisticated test version touched 322mph (515kph) in 1990, a feat that will remain unchallenged from this side of the Channel for a good while yet. The Eurostar's performance as it shot through the Nashenden Valley, south of Rochester, brought a much-needed glow of comfort to its loss-making operator and the entire British railway industry.

Passenger services on the 44-mile Channel Tunnel express link, the country's first new main line for more than a century, will begin at the end of September.

Trains will run at a typically sedate average pace of 30mph between Waterloo and the start of the express route at Fawkham before accelerating to 186mph (300kph), cutting 20 minutes from the current journey to Paris.

The French capital will be two hours 35 minutes away, while travel times to Brussels will drop to two hours 20 minutes . . .

Britain becomes the fifth European country to join the 300kph club, following France, Germany, Belgium and Spain. The driver of Train 3134, Alan Pears, said it was "very exciting" to set a new standard for the British industry. "I had no doubts we were going to do it, and it felt very good," said Mr. Pears, 35, of Staplehurst, Kent.

"I do these kind of speeds on the Continent all the time, but to do it in Kent with countryside I know flashing past was something special."
. . .

The Eurostar train, unlike its renowned predecessors, . . . owes more to overseas design than British. It is largely based on the French Trains Grand Vitesse.

Paul Marston
Transport Correspondent
The Daily Telegraph,
31st July 2003

The following exercises will help you to see what you should consider in the examination when you are given an article to analyse. You can check your answers for all the exercises on page 81.

Photographs

1 Comment on the sequence and organisation of the images used ....

....

....

2 Compare the choice of camera angle and background in each of the photographs and

comment on why the photograph was taken in this way ....

....

....

Headlines

1. **Position** Where are the headlines placed on the page?	3. **Language** Pick out a word with metaphorical meaning; and a phrase that is alliterative. What added effect does the use of these words have on the headline?
2. **Size** Are the headlines large or small or medium-sized?	4. **Information** What information does the headline give?

Quick Tip!

* It can be useful to go through each paragraph of the article highlighting the key words to isolate the important facts. For example, the words 'shattered the 200mph barrier' in the first paragraph of the article on page 33.

Content

1 What type of information is given in the captions under the photographs?

....

2 Which country is the 'competitor' in this 'race'? ....

3 What is the effect of this new achievement for passengers? ....

....

4 What **negative** information is given, suggesting that perhaps it is not a complete

triumph? ....

....

5 Give two examples of 'lesser details'.

a) ....

b) ....

Use of language

1 How many of the five 'Ws' are present in the first paragraph of the article on page 33 and what are they? ....

....

2 Give two examples of emotive language ....

....

3 What do they add to the article? ....

....

....

4 Give two examples of factual language ....

....

5 What does the use of the first person add to the article? ....

....

....

 When you have finished, compare your answers with those on page 81.

 Now do the practice examination question below. You will have 40 minutes to do this question in the exam so time yourself carefully when doing it.

Quick Tip!

✱ Read the question carefully and make sure you answer **all** the bullet points. Try to leave five minutes at the end to check:

a) your spelling and grammar

b) that you have given the correct facts/quotes from the article.

EXAM PRACTICE QUESTION

Read the article on page 33 from *The Daily Telegraph* '208mph: In the tracks of Rocket and Mallard, Eurostar breaks British Record'. How successful is the article in describing the achievement of the Eurostar?

In your answer you should comment on:

✱ the content of the article

✱ the use of headlines

✱ the use of photographs

✱ the use of language in the first-hand accounts

✱ any other features of layout and design.

Leaflets

There are many uses for leaflets – they may give information, such as the kind you find in doctors' surgeries, or they may be advertising something. In the examination you will be asked whether a leaflet makes an **effective** impact on the reader. To do this you will need to consider:

* the layout and design – fonts, design features, organisation on page

* headings and captions

* photographs and diagrams

* the information included

* the tone and use of language.

For instance in the left-hand side picture of the leaflet on the next page:

* What strikes you immediately about the people in the picture? (Photographs)

* Do their faces look at all familiar? Who might they be? (Photographs)

* What heading stands out the most and why? (Headings)

* What information is given? Is it clear? (Information)

On the right-hand side you are given the DOs and DON'Ts of 'surviving' street performers.

* What is the tone of these comments – are they amusing or factual? Write one down. Is it suitable for the subject? (Tone)

* Are they negative or positive? Write an example down. (Tone)

* Do you think the layout is clear? How does it 'draw' you to read it? (Layout)

Inside this leaflet are photographs and a description of the street performers you might expect to see.

* Would you like to look inside to see what is 'on offer'?

* Do you think the language used would be amusing or solemn?

* What would you expect to find in the photographs? Would they be lively or a 'straight' picture of the people involved?

 EXAM PRACTICE QUESTION

Using the above information to help you, answer the following question.

'Do you think this leaflet is an **effective** advertisement and if so, why?'

Quick Tip!

* Organise yourself to take 40 minutes on this essay, as it is all the time you will have in the exam. Plan for five minutes, write for 30 minutes and then check it over for spelling and grammar, etc. for the final five minutes.

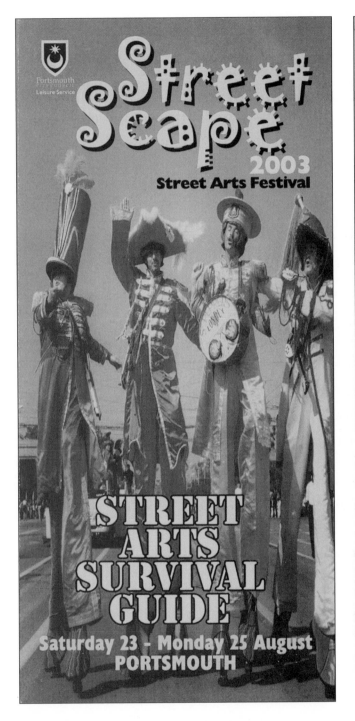

DO's & DON'T's

How to survive being set upon by street performers

In the event of a street performance there are a few things which can greatly increase your chances of survival. Follow these handy hints to ensure maximum enjoyment!...

DO GATHER TOGETHER WITH AS MANY PASSERS BY AS POSSIBLE TO SURROUND THE STREET PERFORMERS AND STOP THEM ESCAPING

DON'T BE AFRAID TO LAUGH AT STREET PERFORMERS - IT'S WHAT THEY GET PAID FOR!

DO MAKE LOUD NOISES BY WAVING YOUR ARMS ABOUT AND SLAPPING THE PALMS OF YOUR HANDS TOGETHER

DO BE PREPARED TO VOLUNTEER YOURSELF FOR PUBLIC RIDICULE

DON'T RUN AWAY. STREET ARTISTS CAN RUN AS FAST AS CHEETAHS - EVEN WHEN RIDING A UNICYCLE

And finally **DO** enjoy yourself!

And remember, if you see any crocodiles then wrestle them to the ground - they are not part of the programme!

Street Arts is a vibrant emerging artform in the UK today

It is a lively and direct expression of contemporary culture that connects with people in their everyday environment - the street. Sometimes chaotic, often hilarious, street performances are an immediate interaction between artists and passers-by which transform spaces into theatres, street corners into stages and ordinary days into extraordinary experiences. Streetscape 2003 proves that the arts are as relevant, inclusive and accessible at street level as they are in any theatre, art gallery or concert hall.

SECTION B: WRITING

Introduction to Revising the 'Writing Triplets'

You will be required to write in **three** of the **nine** genres:

* Argue, Persuade, Advise

* Inform, Explain, Describe

* Analyse, Review, Comment

that is, **one** from each group. So why revise them all?

Simple:

1 There is always a choice of **two** questions, but with **three** possible topics, obviously one will be left out.

2 That one (e.g. Advise) may be the one you revised!

3 You may not like the two options which remain ...

4 SO:

* do yourself a favour, and have a look at them all

* also look back at some of the work you did on them, especially in Year 11

* sort out in your mind what they all mean.

You **could** be asked to write in various genres, e.g. a business or personal letter, an article, speech, leaflet, report and so on.

SO make sure that you know the **format** and **layout** for each one.

Also consider:
    WHO is the target **audience/recipient**?
    WHAT is the real **purpose** of the writing?

Enter into the spirit of the thing and try to make your writing:

* realistic

* believable

* convincing.

Good Luck!

⑤ Writing to Argue, Persuade, Advise

Writing to Argue

If you can do this well, you will have learned a very valuable life-skill or two:

* how to state your case
* how to get your own way/win the day!

Note, however, that it is in **writing** and not in discussion, so don't deliberately argue with your friends and think you're revising for your exams!

The examiner will be looking for:

* evidence of your **reasoning**
* a **clear** writing style
* a **logical sequence** to your points
* a definite, summarising **conclusion**.

The chances are that you will be given a **basic proposition**, such as: 'The school leaving age should be raised from 16 to 18' or: 'People spend too much time watching television instead of doing something active' and will be asked to ARGUE either FOR or AGAINST it. This is rather like some of the debating you may have done for Speaking and Listening, especially if it is a speech you are asked to write.

Remember to:

* think **QUICKLY** and **CLEARLY** about which side to take
* make a few notes before beginning
* make sure you set it out correctly in the genre required (e.g. don't forget the two addresses if it's a business letter)
* try to leave time to check it over at the end.

Quick Tips!

* Keep to the 40 minute time slot!
* Punctuation and spelling DO matter!

 EXAM PRACTICE QUESTION

Your school, in order to make extra money for books and computers, has agreed to host a telephone mast. Some people are not happy about this and a public meeting has been called. Certain pupils from Years 11–13 have been asked to give the pupils' viewpoint. Write the speech you would give either **for** or **against** the mast. Spend 40 minutes on this.

Begin with 'Ladies and gentlemen, parents, staff and pupils . . .'

End with 'And that, ladies and gentlemen, is why we **can't have/must have** this mast.'

 **EXAM PRACTICE QUESTION**

a) Pick two to three of the following **propositions** and write five points arguing **for** and five points **against** each one:
   ✱ 'Pupils should be able to write reports on teachers.'
   ✱ 'Homework should be abolished!'
   ✱ 'Money is the root of all evil.'
   ✱ 'Marriage is outdated.'
   ✱ 'The computer has caused more problems than it has solved.'
   ✱ 'All drugs should now be legalised.'

b) Now choose **one** of your propositions and develop it further.
   ✱ Decide **for** or **against** it.
   ✱ Write an **opening** paragraph, making one or two main points.
   ✱ **Itemise** the other points (four to six) that you would include in the next two to three paragraphs but **do not** write them.
   ✱ Now write the **concluding** paragraph, briefly summing up your whole argument.

Quick Tips!

   ✱ Stick to **reasons**.
   ✱ Keep off **feelings**.
   ✱ Try to **win** the argument!

Writing to Persuade

There's no constraint here about **how** you persuade, so long as you do it effectively! You're probably rather good at the art of persuasion in your everyday life, so bring your powers to bear on the exam paper!

Think of the last time you **persuaded** someone to give in to your view on something, or your request for something. How did you do it?

Was it by:

✱ putting forward good supporting reasons?

✱ gentle arm-twisting?

✱ appealing to their emotions?

✱ subtle blackmail?

✱ threatening or promising something?

The list could be endless!

Which group of people are clever professional persuaders? **Advertisers**, of course!

See how you match up by doing the exercise below. You only have ten minutes to do it in!

Imagine that you have left school and are working for an advertising agency. You have been asked to word an advertisement for what **sounds** like an almost impossible product:

Black, onion-flavoured toothpaste!

The manufacturers want to aim it at young people. They suggest that it needs a short zappy name, such as 'Wow!', 'Zing' or 'Zap'. You have a maximum of 25 words for your advertisement.

See what you can do! Then:

✱ read it over to yourself. Would **you** be persuaded to buy it?
✱ if not, make some alterations!
✱ check your **adjectives** carefully
✱ make some free offers!
✱ show its advantages over ordinary, boring toothpaste.

 EXAM PRACTICE QUESTION

Do **one** of the following activities.

a) You have an old friend who has recently been cautioned then arrested for football hooliganism. Write a **persuasive letter** or e-mail to try to make him see that his behaviour brings the game he says he loves into disrepute. Use any form of persuasion you think necessary.

b) Write a **persuasive article** for a sports magazine defending skate-boarding against the accusation that it is not a real sport.

 EXAM PRACTICE QUESTION

Do **one** of the following activities.

a) Structure a **playscript** in which you persuade one of your reluctant parents to allow you to adopt a hairstyle they find absolutely outrageous.

b) Your local paper has invited readers to suggest how a piece of waste land in your area could be developed for the benefit of residents. Write a **persuasive letter** suggesting that a drop-in centre for young people (including computer facilities, dancing and a non-alcoholic bar) would make the most sense, as there is currently nowhere for them to go.

Show your letter to a friend or member of your family. Ask them:
✱ How persuasive is it?
✱ How could it be made more persuasive?

Then have another go!

Writing to Advise

Giving advice is always a delicate matter, whether it is:

* personal   * practical   * professional.

It should, however, always be:

* clear   * sympathetic (if personal)   * easy to follow (if practical).

In writing, it will usually take the form of:

* a letter   * an e-mail

* a report   * an article

* a leaflet   * a speech/talk.

Make sure that you are comfortable and familiar with each of the genres, including layout and structure.

 EXAM PRACTICE QUESTION

> '...85% of smokers start between the ages of 11–24. The earlier you start the harder it is to stop. Teenagers are particularly vulnerable: due to peer pressure, wanting to be seen as 'cool' or grown up, and (girls especially) using smoking as a form of weight-control.
>
> Nicotine is a powerful drug which soon creates dependency. It also dramatically increases the risks of heart disease, lung cancer and stroke. It can reduce normal life expectancy by up to 20 years ...'

Imagine that you have a friend your own age who is a fairly regular smoker. Using the information in the article and any other ideas of your own, write a letter advising him or her to give up.

 EXAM PRACTICE QUESTION

Do **two** of the following activities.

a) Your local radio station is currently running a series of programmes about the lives of young people in the area. Drawing on your own experience, you have been selected to advise Year 10 and 11 students on how to get the best out of their work experience programmes. Write the **script** of the **ten minute talk** you would give.

b) Edexcel has organised a competition for a **leaflet** entitled, 'How to Do Well in Your Exams!'. The winning leaflet will be used in the Board's publicity material next year. Write your entry.

Remember:
* leaflets use pictograms as well as words   * use bullet points, capitals etc. for emphasis
* make it student-friendly   * keep it clear.

c) Write an **advice sheet** for first year university/college students living away from home. Include such things as: making a simple, balanced meal; social life; keeping up with the work; staying in touch with home, and other ideas of your own.

d) Write some **safety advice** for teenage helpers at a summer camp who will be teaching young children to swim, cycle, horse-ride, skateboard, and so on.

     * You can include lists of DOs and DON'Ts!

6 Writing to Inform, Explain, Describe

Writing to Inform

Informing, like describing, is a constant human activity, of which you will, by now, have had vast experience! Think about how often you are asked to give basic information about yourself: name, address, age, telephone number, e-mail. More complex information about yourself, for example your plans for the next ten years, requires a more complex answer. It also requires more **organisation** and needs to be:

✱ clear   ✱ direct   ✱ relevant   ✱ precise.

 EXAM PRACTICE QUESTION

All the leaving Year 11 students have been asked to contribute details about themselves and their school careers (in 500–700 words) for a School Year Book, to be desk-top published by the school in the autumn. The Head has not given a format for the entries in order to encourage an individual approach by each student.

Think about:
✱ **what** to include (e.g. some facts, some anecdotes)
✱ **how** to present it (style, layout etc.)
✱ **which** language register to use (e.g. formal, colloquial, a mixture of both).

Plan how to (briefly):
✱ write notes on the above
✱ put them into paragraph order
✱ keep within the word limit.

Then – **Write it up!**

Quick Tip!

✱ When in doubt, leave it out!

 EXAM PRACTICE QUESTION

Do **two** of the following activities.

a) Imagine that you have a temporary summer job in the local Tourist Office. They have asked you to research and write an **information sheet** on the 'Entertainment, Leisure and Sports Facilities' in your area. Write the sheet you would present to them.

Remember:
✱ use sub-headings
✱ give addresses and directions
✱ try to make it easy-to-follow
✱ keep the tone impartial (don't show any negative or positive bias).

b) Your French teacher has established a pen-friend scheme with a school in Paris. You have been allocated a pen-friend called Pierre, aged 15. Write your first letter to him (in English, of course!) giving **information** about yourself, your home, school etc. that you think he will find of interest.

c) Write about one of your favourite activities or sports for a reference book entry of 500 words, for example, 'DANCING is great fun, keeps you fit, and is a good way of meeting people . . .'

Remember:
* give **information** about it
* keep it lively and interesting
* use appropriate detail, e.g. any equipment necessary
* aim it at the general reader.

d) A close friend regularly watches the same 'soap' as you (e.g. *EastEnders* or *Neighbours*) but missed the last episode and was unable to video it. **Inform** him or her about what happened in a personal letter, an e-mail or telephone conversation (playscripted).

Remember:
* write as full an account as possible
* use the right layout/format for your chosen genre
* make it as chatty/realistic as possible.

Writing to Explain

'**Explain** what you mean .., **Explain** where you were . . . **Explain** how to do it . . .'. These are all often demanded by others, sometimes to our annoyance; yet explaining things is one of the things we do best.

For the purposes of this exam, you **could** be asked to explain:

* a situation (real or imagined)
* a choice you have made and its outcome
* your feelings about something
* your views on a particular issue
* some aspect of your experience.

The examiner will be looking for ideas that:

* are well thought out
* are expressed in a suitable/logical order
* are expressed in a confident, easy style
* have correct grammar, punctuation or spelling
* have some humour, where appropriate.

Imagine that this is the 'Explain' option of two questions on the paper:

'Explain what you hope to do with the next five years of your life.'

How do you go about it? Clearly, you **could** answer it in a paragraph:

'After GCSEs I hope to go on to AS and A2 for two years, then go to a good university for three years, then perhaps do an MA or MBA, then get a good job earning a lot of money by the time I'm 25.'

But that is clearly unsatisfactory. Why?
* The 'facts' are too baldly stated.
* There are no interesting details.
* There are no answers to the 'Why?' of it.
* It is poorly written (three 'thens', all in one sentence).
* It's boring!

Quick Tip!

* Remember, the examiners have given you 40 minutes to answer this question and don't want something you finish in five minutes!

Here is a re-structuring of the opening:

'After GCSEs in eight subjects, I hope to go on to AS and A2 in (give subjects) because (give reasons). At the same time, I intend to develop my out of school interests in (explain what) and take up (decide what). I think this will give me an all-round development.'

EXAM PRACTICE QUESTION

a) Using the same example as above, write your own first paragraph of this answer, making sure that you **explain** your reasons.

b) Then **map out** (in note form) the middle two to three paragraphs, along the same lines.

c) Write the **last** paragraph in full.

Remember: It doesn't all have to be strictly **true** but it has to be a good answer to the question!

Choose **two** of the following:

a) Explain the **plot** of any literature text you have read for GCSE and say why it's worth reading.

b) Explain your **views** about student fees and loans for living expenses, and your **feelings** about possibly taking these on yourself.

c) Think of a place you have been to fairly recently that surprised or excited you and explain why it made such an impact on you.

Then:
* Do a quick plan (five minutes maximum).
* Time yourself 30 minutes' **writing time.**
* STOP!
* Spend five minutes checking and correcting.
* Do the other one tomorrow, using the same timings.

Writing to Describe

Describing is what we do most of the time!

For example, we might describe:

* a person we met
* a place we went to
* something that happened to us
* an object we've bought
* a film/book/play/CD, etc.

Much of our describing is spoken, in our everyday lives. Trying to do it effectively in writing requires more discipline and planning.

FIRSTLY: decide which **aspects** of the person, place, event or object you wish to convey.
SECONDLY: think of the **details** you wish to show.
THIRDLY: consider the best **language** to use.
FOURTHLY: balance the **factual** and **imaginative** elements.

Also, try to be aware of your **audience** and **purpose.**

For example, if you were asked to write an article entitled, 'The Best and Worst of School: A Leaver's View', for the school magazine, it would be quite different from an article of the same title written for *The Times Educational Supplement* (TES), a newspaper for teachers. Your **audience** and **purpose** would be different:

* the school magazine would try to **entertain** and be a bit irreverent, and might use more colloquial language;

* the TES article would be more serious, less jokey and written in standard English.

In both versions, however, in the course of **describing** your experiences, you would also have to **explain** and give **information** because your material would be basically **factual**.

 EXAM PRACTICE QUESTION

Imagine that you have recently been to one of these places:
* a busy airport
* the first day of the sales
* an FA Cup Final.

Describe what you saw, heard, felt, and the other people present (how did they show their pleasure or frustration?). Choose your language to suit your purpose.

Read over and correct what you have written. Would you write it differently if it was the opening paragraph of a story?

In a more **imaginative** description, you would put more emphasis on:
* creating atmosphere
* conveying feelings
* choice of adjectives and verbs
* use of imagery (metaphors and similes).

 EXAM PRACTICE QUESTION

a) In about 6–8 lines, describe one of these:
   * a thunderstorm
   * first winter snow
   * a starry night
   * a fine spring morning.

   Remember to use similes and metaphors, as well as good adjectives and verbs.

b) Describe your own home so as to create a mental 'photograph' of it, dwelling particularly on the parts of it you are specially fond of or which have a special meaning for you.

Quick Tips!

* Try to pick out 'telling' details.

* **Vary** your choice of adjectives and **avoid** meaningless ones (e.g. wonderful/great).

Writing to Analyse, Review, Comment

UNIT 7

Writing to Analyse

This clearly overlaps with **argue** and **explain** and to a lesser extent with **describe**. It really means **examine something in-depth**, probing what it's really about. Sherlock Holmes used the analytical method to solve cases which baffled the police, and scientists analyse the nature and function of matter, liquids, gasses etc.

For the purposes of this exam, 'Writing to Analyse' often means examining two sides of a question, for example 'Is it better to take holidays abroad or in Britain?' or 'Is the examination system the best way of showing people's abilities?'.

Examining both sides of a question needs:

* balanced judgement   * freedom from obvious bias   * personal detachment.

Whereas 'Writing to Argue' usually just tries to prove one view to be the best.

EXAM PRACTICE QUESTION

Consider the following question: 'Write about the advantages and disadvantages of living in a city or large town.'

It is important, **before** beginning, to:

* think of/note down points on both sides   * decide what you think yourself

* try to get a balance of views   * try not to let this bias your answer.

Now:

* Make a quick list of eight to ten points on both sides.

* Check it with the list on page 82.

* Use whatever combination of the two suits you best.

Then:

a) Work these points into 3–4 **mid-essay** paragraphs, but **don't** write the **opening** or **concluding** paragraphs yet because they serve a different purpose . . .

b) When you've done **a)**, think about what you've written:

* are the points balanced or have you got more on one side?

* if so, try to even it up.

c) **Now** consider the **opening** paragraph. It should consist of some **general points** on the subject, before you go into your advantages and disadvantages. Keep it to 6–8 lines. (See example on page 82.)

d) **Then** consider the **conclusion:** this should sum up your **main points** and (if you wish) give your own personal view.

 **EXAM PRACTICE QUESTION**

Choose **two** of the following and time yourself **strictly** to 40 minutes each.

a) It has been said that your generation are more interested in computer games than field games. Consider the arguments for and against this view.

b) Analyse the pros and cons of co-educational as opposed to single-sex schools. Which would you prefer yourself, and why?

c) Analyse your own experience of the present exam system and suggest how you think it could be improved.

d) What, in your view, makes a really good teacher?

Writing to Review

Broadly speaking, this includes taking a long look at things, people or activities and considering what we think of them. When it comes to writing reviews of films/books/plays/concerts and so on, they are usually **critical**, that is, trying to assess their worth.

A review can also be your **further** thoughts on something you have thought about before. Exam questions are likely to be experience-based e.g. you may be asked to **review** some aspect of your own life, school or area. At least you don't have to revise for that – you know it already! What you **may** need to revise, though, is **how** to do it.

For example, if you were given the following question:

'Write a review of the last film you saw that you thought was really good (whether on video or at the cinema).'

How would you go about it? What would you include? What would you omit?

'Review' means take an overall look at:

* the basic plot-line
* the characterisation
* particularly striking incidents
* the acting

* locations/setting
* music at different times
* photography (long shots, close-ups etc.)
* anything else that occurs to you.

Don't be afraid to be critical too, if there were also parts/things that you **didn't** like.

 **EXAM PRACTICE QUESTION**

When you've had five to ten minutes to decide the film and gather your thoughts together, time yourself 30–35 minutes to actually **write** the review.

Use the heading:

'A Review of '..**' starring** ....

EXAM PRACTICE QUESTION

Choose **two** of the following activities:

a) You have probably considered a number of possible jobs/careers. Review your recent thoughts on the subject, with reasons, explaining your latest idea or most likely course of action.

b) Review your last two years at school, under headings such as: Academic Progress, Social Life, Sports/Interests, Responsibilities, Achievements, Best/Worst Moments and any other categories of your own.

c) Imagine that you have left school and have been asked to review your school experiences from 5–16/18 years old for a magazine article entitled, 'The Best and Worst of School'. (See also 'Writing to Describe' on page 45.) Write the article you would submit to the editor.

d) Review the recent progress of one of your favourite singers/groups **or** sportsperson.

When you have made your choices, do a quick five minute plan for each one.

Then set yourself 35 minutes to write **one** of them, leaving five minutes to check it at the end.

Writing to Comment

We are always commenting on things, just by passing remarks, or making observations. There are many ways of commenting: for example a sports commentator describes and **comments** on the action of a game; the Chorus in a Greek tragedy stood near the actors and **commented** on the action of the play.

It overlaps with **describing, explaining,** and **reviewing** and is very much about your **own opinion** of something. For example, if you were asked to **comment** on your last evening's television viewing, it would be a mixture of:

✱ facts/information
                          = commentary.
✱ your own opinion

It would need:

✱ structure (a plan or shape)

✱ details (carefully selected)

✱ a brief introduction – and conclusion.

EXAM PRACTICE QUESTION

Write a letter to a friend who has been abroad for a few months, informing him or her of what has been happening in your life at home and at school, **commenting** on particular achievements, plans or problems.

Quick Tip!

✱ Try to make it sound authentic, even if it's pure fiction! (It's not a 'truth test', it's an exam strategy!)

EXAM PRACTICE QUESTION

Choose **one** of the following activities:

a) Write a detailed **commentary** on a book, TV programme, play or concert that you have recently enjoyed.

b) Write an account of a recent holiday for a travel magazine, **commenting** on the place(s), the people, hotel or other accommodation, the activities and facilities available, local food, night life and anything else you think would interest people who have never been there but might consider going. (Your comments do **not** all have to be favourable.)

* Decide which option you prefer.
* Do a brief plan for your answer (five minutes maximum).
* Time yourself 35 minutes.
* Write it!
* If possible (within the time limit) check it over for mistakes.
* Leave it for a few hours or days, then re-read it.

ASK YOURSELF:

1 How much useful information did it convey?

2 Was it written in an engaging, interesting way?

3 Was the actual commentary:
  * detailed enough?
  * fair overall?
  * useful to others?
  * your considered opinion?

If you can honestly answer YES to all these and someone else has read it and agrees with you – well done! If not, or not entirely – have another go!

SECTION C: LITERATURE

Introduction to Section C: Literature

The format for Section C: Literature is as follows:

* Post-1914 Prose (Unit 8, page 52)

* Post-1914 Drama (Unit 9, page 59)

* Literary Non-fiction (Unit 10, page 65)

The following are the areas on which exam questions will be based. Remember, you will also be examined on poetry. This is covered in Section A of this Revision guide.

* themes/moral attitudes

* characters and their roles and development

* characters and their relationships with other characters

* plot/events

* atmosphere and settings

* key quotes/speeches.

Quick Tips!

* **Highlight** the different sections of a question to make sure you answer every part.

* Keep referring back to the question when writing your essay to make sure that you respond to **all** parts of it.

  MARKS ARE LOST if you do **NOT** answer **ALL** of the question.

* Support your answer with reference to the text or by use of a **brief** quote.

* Bear in mind that long quotes do not gain more marks and waste valuable writing time.

 **8** # Post-1914 Prose

Themes and Moral Attitudes

Themes

These are the underlying or unifying ideas which appear throughout the text. They reflect aspects of the book's main subject and the author's purpose. Look at the example below.

TEXT:	*To Kill a Mockingbird*
Theme:	**Racial disharmony**

SECONDARY THEMES
- Rites of passage/growing up.
- One good man against the world.
- Appearance and reality.

Moral attitudes

Look for the following:

✱ moral attitude of a major character (e.g. Atticus)

✱ a different character who shows a different moral standpoint (e.g. Ewell)

✱ moral attitude of the author (e.g. racial harmony is superior to racial intolerance).

 In the box below write out examples/quotations from the text that you are studying, illustrating the above.

TEXT:	Quotations
1 Its main theme:	
2 Secondary themes:	
3 Moral attitudes of a main character:	
4 Find a different view in the text:	
5 Moral attitude of the author:	

Characters: Their Roles and Development

Main characters

In note-form complete the chart below for **one** of the main characters in the text you have studied and compare your answer with the example given on page 83. Then repeat this exercise for another main character.

TEXT:	Character:

APPEARANCE

PERSONALITY

ROLE IN TEXT

CHANGE AND DEVELOPMENT OF CHARACTER IN THE COURSE OF THE BOOK

Quick Tip!

✱ Show your knowledge of the text by using a **brief** quote to support your response.

Now do the same for two or three secondary characters (if there are any) but only including Appearance and Personality.

Relationships between characters

Complete the following table showing the relationships between two major characters, for example George and Lenny in *Of Mice and Men*.

Quick Tip!

✱ Make **brief** notes and remember a **short** quote is more effective.

TEXT:	Characters:
AT THE BEGINNING OF THE BOOK	
IN THE MIDDLE OF THE BOOK	
AT THE END OF THE BOOK	

 If you are studying *Of Mice and Men*, compare your answers with those on page 83.

 Fill in the boxes below showing the relationship, where appropriate, between a major and a less important character, for example George and the girl in *Of Mice and Men*.

TEXT:	Characters:
AT THE BEGINNING OF THE BOOK	
IN THE MIDDLE OF THE BOOK	
AT THE END OF THE BOOK	

Plot

The plot is shown in its sequence of events and in its twists and surprises. Some plots are 'open-ended', whilst others come to a definite unravelling or resolution.

Think about a book that you have read and fill in the following table by:
1 Picking out six main parts of the plot.
2 Finding (brief!) key quotes for each part.
3 Write about one major event in more detail and show its importance in your text. Spend 40 minutes on this.

TEXT:	Key quotes
1 OPENING SITUATION	
2 FIRST MAJOR EVENT	
3 FURTHER COMPLICATIONS	
4 CRISIS POINT(S)	
5 TENSION OR SUSPENSE	
6 HOW IT ALL ENDS	

Atmosphere and Setting

Complete the following table, using examples and quotations from the text you are studying, for example *Animal Farm*.

TEXT:	
1 How does the writer create the atmosphere at the beginning of the story?	
2 How does the writer set the scene?	
3 How does the writer show changes early in the story?	
4 How do the characters respond to/help create the atmosphere?	
5 How believable is the atmosphere created by the writer?	
6 Where else in the story does the atmosphere change?	
7 What is the atmosphere at the end of the text and how has it changed from the beginning?	

Time:

✱ Historical time: Past, Present, Future.

✱ Shifts in time (e.g. flashbacks).   **Time + Place = Setting**

✱ Significant moments.

Place: Physical place. Can you visualise it from the author's description? Is it real?
Setting: is both Historical and Cultural and Geographical.

1 How are the settings suitable for the story?	
2 Are there multiple settings? Give details:	
3 What does the setting add: a) to our understanding of the characters? b) to the atmosphere?	

When you have finished, compare your answers with those on page 84.

Key Quotes/Speeches

1 Complete the following table using quotations from the text you are studying.

Characters	Themes	Atmosphere	Setting
1			**HISTORICAL CULTURAL**
2			**GEOGRAPHICAL**
3			**LOCATIONS**

2 Find a quotation which seems to most sum up the book ....

....

3 Find a quotation which could be misleading and say why ....

....

EXAM PRACTICE QUESTION

Write about the relationship between any **two** key characters in your novel and how they affect the outcome of the book. You have 40 minutes in which to complete your answer.

Quick Tip!

✱ Don't go over the time – you can't in the exam!

Language and Interpretation

This is a useful revision aid that you might want to use for all of the prose pieces that you are revising.

 Complete the following table for the text you are studying.

TEXT:

1 **What narrative voice is used: first or third person?**

2 **What impression do we gain of the narrator from the opening sentences/paragraphs?**

3 **Sentences: give examples of the use of variation of length and pace and comment on the effects achieved.**

4 **Find a complex sentence with several clauses and comment on the effect achieved.**

5 **Find a subordinate clause and comment on its effect.**

6 **Paragraphs: comment on variation of length and effects achieved.**

7 **Find examples of imagery and figurative language and comment on the effects achieved.**

8 **Find examples where language is used to create mood or atmosphere and comment on how the effect is achieved.**

9 **Find examples of humour and irony and say how the author uses language to achieve tone.**

9 Post-1914 Drama

Themes and Moral Attitudes

These are the underlying or unifying ideas which appear throughout the text. They reflect aspects of the play's main subject and the playwright's purpose. Look at the example below.

TEXT: *An Inspector Calls*
Main theme: Appearance and reality
SECONDARY THEMES • Moral responsibility. • 'Whodunnit'. • The seven deadly sins. • The British class system.

Moral attitudes

Look for the following:

✱ moral attitude of a major character (e.g. Arthur Birling)

✱ a different character who shows a different moral standpoint (e.g. Inspector Goole)

✱ moral attitude of the author (e.g. beneath the smug middle class surface lie dark secrets and moral guilt).

 In the box below write out examples/quotations from the text that you are studying, illustrating the above.

TEXT:	Quotations
1 Its main theme:	
2 Secondary themes:	
3 Moral attitudes of a main character:	
4 A different view in the text:	
5 Moral attitude of the author:	

Characters: Their Roles and Development

Main characters

In note-form complete the chart below for **one** of the main characters in the play you have studied and compare your answer with the example given on page 85. Then repeat this exercise for another main character.

TEXT:	Character:

APPEARANCE

PERSONALITY

ROLE IN TEXT

CHANGE AND DEVELOPMENT OF CHARACTER IN THE COURSE OF THE PLAY

Quick Tip!

✱ Show your knowledge of the text by using a **brief** quote to support your response.

 Now do the same for two or three secondary characters (if there are any) but only include Appearance and Personality.

Relationships between characters

Complete the following table showing the relationships between two major characters (for example Arthur and Eric Birling in *An Inspector Calls*).

Quick Tip!

✱ Use **brief** notes and **short** quotes!

TEXT:	Characters:
AT THE BEGINNING OF THE PLAY/IN ACT 1	
IN THE MIDDLE OF THE PLAY/IN ACT 2	
AT THE END OF THE PLAY/IN ACT 3	

If you are studying *An Inspector Calls* compare your answers with those on page 85.

Fill in the boxes below showing the relationship, where appropriate, between a major and a less important character, for example Sheila Birling and Gerald Croft.

TEXT:	Characters:
AT THE BEGINNING OF THE PLAY/IN ACT 1	
IN THE MIDDLE OF THE PLAY/IN ACT 2	
AT THE END OF THE PLAY/IN ACT 3	

Quick Tip!

✱ Do **NOT** use page numbers (e.g. 'See Birling, middle p.33') because different editions have different page numbers!

Plot

The plot of a play is shown in its sequence of events and in their twists and surprises. Some are 'open-ended' (e.g. *An Inspector Calls*), whilst others come to a definite unravelling of the plot or resolution (e.g. *Educating Rita*).

1 Thinking of the play that you have studied, fill in the following table by picking out six main parts of the plot.
2 Find key quotes for each part.
3 Write about one major event in more detail and show its importance in your text.

TEXT:	Key Quotes
1 OPENING SITUATION	
2 FIRST MAJOR EVENT	
3 FURTHER COMPLICATIONS	
4 CRISIS POINT(S)	
5 TENSION OR SUSPENSE	
6 HOW IT ALL ENDS	

Quick Tip!

* Keep your quotes brief!

Atmosphere and Setting

Complete the following table, using examples and quotations from the text you are studying (for example *An Inspector Calls*).

TEXT:	
1 How does the writer create the atmosphere at the beginning of the play?	
2 How does the writer set the scene?	
3 How does the writer show changes early in the play?	
4 How do the characters respond to/help create the atmosphere?	
5 How believable is the atmosphere created by the writer?	
6 Where else in the play does the atmosphere change?	
7 What is the atmosphere at the end of the text and how has it changed from the beginning?	

Time:

✳ Historical time: Past, Present, Future.

✳ Shifts in time (e.g. flashbacks).　　　　**Time + Place = Setting**

✳ Significant moments.

Place: Physical place. Can you visualise it from the author's description? Is it real?
Setting: is both Historical and Cultural and Geographical.

Answer the following, using examples from the text:

1 How are the settings suitable for the play?	
2 Are there multiple settings? Give details:	
3 What does the setting add: 　a) to our understanding of the characters? 　b) to the atmosphere?	

When you have finished compare your answers with those on page 86.

Key Quotes/Speeches

 1 Complete the following table using quotations from the text you are studying.

Characters	Themes	Atmosphere	Setting
1			**HISTORICAL/ CULTURAL**
2			**GEOGRAPHICAL**
3			**LOCATIONS**

2 Find a quotation which seems to most sum up the play ....

....

3 Find a quotation which could be misleading and say why ....

....

 EXAM PRACTICE QUESTION

The essence of drama is conflict: write about the conflict in your play and how it is resolved. You have 40 minutes in which to complete your answer.

Quick Tip!

✱ Don't go over the time – you can't in the exam!

Literary Non-fiction
English Literature (1213 Paper 2F or 3H)

The texts in this unit are autobiographies, personal histories, memoirs or narrative journalism.

Remember:

* events and characters are seen through the author's eyes
* we only get the author's viewpoint
* we only see what is included, not what is left out
* we can get a more objective viewpoint by examining the way the author interacts with other characters.

Does the Author Always Tell the Truth?

Though they are works of non-fiction, think of circumstances where the truth may have been slightly altered or even distorted:

* incidents may have been telescoped or run together for pace and continuity
* they may have been simplified, exaggerated or dramatised to make them more interesting
* they may have been manipulated to show the author in a favourable light
* the author may not have remembered exactly how it was, or have been too young to see the whole picture
* the author may have had a political purpose (Orwell, for example).

Authors try to make us see it their way by establishing their:

* truthfulness/objectivity
* eye for detail and powers of observation
* sensitivity or literary ability.

Complete the chart below, for your text, supplying evidence for these qualities.

TEXT:
TRUTHFULNESS/OBJECTIVITY
EYE FOR DETAIL/POWERS OF OBSERVATION
SENSITIVITY/LITERARY ABILITY

When you have finished, compare your answers with those on page 87.

Look for evidence which shows that other characters may see themselves or their actions differently from the way the author sees them. Find examples from your text.

Quick Tip!

* Think of your text as a work of **creative non-fiction**.

Themes and Moral Attitudes

Themes

There are underlying or unifying ideas which appear throughout the text. They reflect aspects of the book's main subject and the author's purpose. Look at the example below.

TEXT: *Chinese Cinderella*	Theme: Childhood and growing up
SECONDARY THEMES	
• Family life.	• Chinese culture and tradition.
• Discrimination and prejudice.	• Education.

Moral attitudes

Look for the following:

✱ moral attitude of a major character (e.g. Aunt Baba who loves, protects and encourages Adeline)

✱ a different character who shows a different moral standpoint (e.g. Niang who hates Adeline)

✱ moral attitudes of the author (Adeline presents her own youthful viewpoint, one of 'stoical fortitude', patience, courage, optimism in adversity, setback, emotional deprivation and acute loneliness).

1 Using a format like that of the box below, identify themes and quotations from the text you are studying. If you are doing *Chinese Cinderella* you could choose other themes and attitudes than those given above. If you are doing *Anne Frank* you will be able to find other examples than those given below.

2 Explore the main theme of your text, bringing out how it connects with the life experiences of a central character. Spend 40 minutes on this.

TEXT: *The Diary of Anne Frank*	Main theme: Adolescence and coming of age
'I am longing for a kiss, the kiss that is so long in coming. I wonder if all the time he [Peter] regards me as a friend. Am I nothing more?' She is suffering the emotional turmoil of teenage love.	
SECONDARY THEMES	
JEWISH CONSCIOUSNESS/ANTI-SEMITISM: 'Our many Jewish friends are being taken away by the dozen. These people are being treated by the Gestapo without a sense of decency . . . Hitler took away our nationality. In fact, Germans and Jews are the greatest enemies in the world'.	
FAMILY RELATIONSHIPS: Anne chronicles the breakdown of the family spirit, under the pressures of confinement and having to live with outsiders. In Entry 75, she is amazed by all the 'abusive exchanges' that now take place. Her father's mouth is permanently clenched; her mother red-faced; her sister, Margot, has a headache; she herself is 'going completely crackers'. Sometimes they forget who they are quarrelling with and who they are not.	
QUEST FOR IDENTITY AND PERSECUTION FEELING: A good example in Entry 41: 'If I talk, everyone thinks I'm showing off; when I'm silent they think I'm ridiculous; rude if I answer, sly if I get a good idea, lazy if I'm tired, selfish if I eat a mouthful more than I should, stupid, cowardly, crafty etc etc . . . I would like to ask God to give me a different nature'.	

Quick Tip!

✱ If you make a collection of key words that are related to the text's main theme you will be in a better position to understand it.

Characters: Their Roles and Development

Main characters

In note-form complete the chart below for a main character in the book you have studied. If you are studying *Bad Blood*, you can compare your answers with those on page 87.

TEXT:	Character:
APPEARANCE	
PERSONALITY	
ROLE IN TEXT	
CHANGE AND DEVELOPMENT OF CHARACTER IN THE COURSE OF THE BOOK	

1 Now do the same for two or three secondary characters (if there are any) but only include Appearance and Personality.

2 What appears to be your text's central character's outlook on life? Give supporting evidence. Spend 40 minutes on this.

Quick Tip!

* Jot down your first ideas about a character as soon as he or she has been introduced. At the end compare your mature judgements with your first impression.

Relationships between characters

Complete the following table showing the relationships between two major characters, for example in *The Diary of Anne Frank*, Anne and her father.

TEXT:	Characters:
AT THE BEGINNING OF THE BOOK	
LATER IN THE BOOK	
AT THE END OF THE BOOK	

 If you are studying *Anne Frank* compare your answers with those on page 88.

Fill in the boxes below showing the relationship, where appropriate, between a major and a less important character, for example Anne and Peter.

TEXT:	Characters:
AT THE BEGINNING OF THE BOOK	
IN THE MIDDLE OF THE BOOK	
AT THE END OF THE BOOK	

Quick Tip!

✱ A good way of keeping track on character relationships is to use a spider diagram. Write your character's name in the central circle; in the outer circles write down any thoughts or ideas he or she has about other characters. Do the same for different characters and look for connections.

Plot

Although these are works of non-fiction, autobiographies, memoirs, personal histories and narrative journalism, they all have some kind of plot, a sequence of events with twists and surprises and a final outcome. The **plot** can often be charted.

1 Think about a text that you have read and fill in the following table by picking out six main parts of the plot.

2 Find (brief!) key quotes for each part.

3 Write about one major event in more detail and show its importance in your text. Spend 40 minutes on this.

TEXT:	Key Quotes
OPENING SITUATION	
FIRST MAJOR EVENT	
FURTHER COMPLICATIONS	
CRISIS POINT(S)	
TENSION OR SUSPENSE	
HOW IT ALL ENDS	

Quick Tip!

✴ Look for the most exciting section of the plot.

Atmosphere and Setting

Setting

The setting of a text is where and when it takes place. Think of this formula:

Setting = Time + Place

Answer the questions in the table below using examples from your text. An example has been done from *Chinese Cinderella*.

HOW IS THE SETTING AT THE BEGINNING SUITABLE?
The young Adeline and her family live in Tianjin, a city port on the north coast of China, occupied by French soldiers after the 'Opium War'. The 'French Concession' was like 'a little piece of Paris transplanted into the centre of this big Chinese city'. The house was built in French style.

IS THERE MORE THAN ONE SETTING? Give details.
When the Japanese invade, the family move to Shanghai, to a 'big, square, dark-grey concrete building'; the city is a place where 'motor cars, trams, rickshaws, pedicabs and bicycles whizzed by'. Adeline attends a missionary school. Later she is sent to boarding school in Tianjin; and later still to Hong Kong.

WHAT DOES THE SETTING/SENSE OF PLACE ADD TO OUR UNDERSTANDING OF THE CHARACTER?
It explains and describes aspects of Chinese culture, and history, for example Grandmother Nai Nai's bound feet; the Buddhist funeral; the celebration of New Year; the arranged marriage of Big Sister to someone twice her age; the spread of Communism etc., all if which impact on the young Adeline.

Atmosphere

Atmosphere is different from setting. It is a mood or feeling experienced in a particular setting at a particular time.

Complete the following table using examples and quotations from the text you are studying.

1 How does the writer create atmosphere at the beginning?	
2 How do characters respond to or help to change the atmosphere?	
3 What is the atmosphere at the end of the text and how has it changed from the beginning/earlier?	

Quick Tip!

✱ Writers often use sensory descriptions when creating atmosphere. Always bear that in mind.

 EXAM PRACTICE QUESTION

Write an essay exploring the relationship between characters and place in your text. You have 40 minutes in which to complete your answer.

Feelings and Emotions

The writers of the texts in this unit describe the grim reality of the conditions which they either grew up in or, in the case of George Orwell and Laurie Lee, volunteered for.

Take an episode or period from your text and find quotations to illustrate the writer's use of the powerful feelings and emotions listed below. If you are doing *A Moment of War* an example has been done for you below. If you are doing *Down and Out in Paris and London*, when you have finished, compare your answers with those on page 88.

TEXT: *A Moment of War* **by Laurie Lee**

The example is from when Laurie Lee, having walked across the Pyrenees to join the Republican Army, is put in a cellar, mistaken for a spy.

FEAR/FOREBODING
'...in this black icy silence I began to get a sharpening taste of danger'.
'I felt the seal of fate on me'.
'Locked in the dark with Dino ... I drew steadily, as I thought, towards my hour ...'.

HUNGER
For about a week Laurie Lee lived on nothing more than a little bread and watered wine.

COLD/DAMP
'It was damp and very cold, the walls of the cellar limed with ice like spidery veins of lace'.
'I curled up on some damp, mouldy straw'.

LONELINESS
'The cell had a curious, narrow, coffin-like shape...'.
'alone in this buried silence'.
'Lying there, shivering, unvisited, well on into the third day, I was wondering idly what now might happen'.

OTHERS

SECTION D: QUICK TIPS FOR SUCCESS

Tips for Poetry

* Focus on the question.
* Don't just feature-spot. Always say what the **effect** is of a feature.
* Use quotations as evidence to back up your point.
* Add your own commentary to quotations. Say why the quotation supports your point.
* **Never** tell the story.
* Think in terms of **showing** and **illustrating** } not just stating.

Before the Exam

* Work through this book.
* Do as many practice essays as you can and rework them to improve your technique.
* Remember essay plans are almost as useful as essays themselves. Keep a file of your essay plans.
* When you have done a piece of work put it to one side and return to it a few days later. Then see if you can improve it.
* Sometimes it is good to revise with a friend and bounce ideas off each other.
* Keep asking the simple question **why**. **Why** do you feel/think something? **Why** does another person hold a different opinion?

Before the exam be aware of the writer's point of view or how he or she is putting it across through:

* organisation of material
* information included and excluded
* language choices – e.g. sentence types, word choice, imagery.

1. **Revise thoroughly**: know the texts.
2. **Get people** to test you.
3. **Learn** some really useful but brief quotations.
4. **Go** to bed early before exams!
5. **Relax** before going into the exam room/hall.

In the Exam

1. **Read** the exam paper very carefully at least **twice** before starting to write, especially any previously unseen material.
2. If there is a **choice** of questions, choose the one you know most about or can do most easily.
3. **Plan** your answer carefully before beginning.
4. Make sure you answer the **actual question** asked!
5. If it has a number of parts to it, **highlight**, **number** or **underline** them so you don't forget any.
6. Use quote marks when making direct quotations.
7. Keep to the topic of the essay or subject of the question and **don't** go off the point.
8. Try to leave time to check your work.
9. If you find any **factual errors** or other mistakes (e.g. spelling) correct them as quickly as you can.
10. Keep a careful eye

on the time . . .

and don't go over five minutes into the next question.

Collection A: In Such a Time as This

'Half-past Two' by U.A. Fanthorpe (answers to page 1)

'Half-past Two' by U.A. Fanthorpe	
SUBJECT: A child is told off by his teacher and told to stay in the schoolroom until half-past two. He had not been taught how to tell the time and we learn what 'times' were special to him. The poem is about communication between children and adults and the way children use words.	**TONE:** Nostalgia about a childhood memory. **VIEWPOINT:** The adult looks back to a childhood punishment and special moment of growing up.
USEFUL QUOTES: 'He did Something Very Wrong'. 'He knew a lot of time: he knew/Gettinguptime, timeyouwereofftime'. 'He escaped into the clockless land of ever'.	**USE OF LANGUAGE:** **Capital letters** to emphasise words important to the child: 'Very Wrong'. **Words run together** as the child heard them 'Timeformykisstime'. **Personification:** 'the little eyes'; 'two long legs for walking'. **Onomatopoeia:** 'click' gives the sound of the clock (normally 'tick'). **Alliteration:** 'slotted . . . into schooltime' and 'home in time for teatime' emphasise that the child was being timetabled back into normal life. Child's language **poetic** compared to that of teacher who uses prosaic, **colloquial** language: 'Run along or you'll be late'.

'Hide and Seek' by Vernon Scannell (answers to page 3)

1. **What the title suggests:** A game of Hide and Seek.

2. **First idea:** The child remembers what he was told to do, he must 'Call Out. Call loud: "I'm ready…come and find me!"'. He must also be careful that his 'feet aren't sticking out'. We realise that this is the first time he has played Hide and Seek.

3. **Mood/tone created:** There is a feeling of childish excitement and a frisson of slight fear that he might be found: 'Wiser not to risk another shout'.

4. **Later ideas:**
   i The boy's thoughts as he waits are:
   * 'They'll probably be searching/The bushes near the swing.'
   * 'And here they are, whispering at the door'
   * 'Don't breathe. Don't move. Stay dumb.'
   ii The children laugh and suddenly disappear.
   iii The child decides he must stay hidden and they must be thinking he is 'very clever' as they can't find him.

5. **Tension/conflict:** This poem is full of tension, as the child awaits his seekers: 'be careful that your feet aren't sticking out' and particularly the line 'Don't breathe. Don't move. Stay dumb' where the short staccato phrases help to create tension. The conflict he feels shows in, 'don't come out just yet …' until 'I've won!/Here I am!'

6. **Imagery in use:**
   Simile: 'The sacks in the toolshed smell like the seaside.'
   Personification: 'the cold bites through your coat'; 'The darkening garden watches'; 'bushes hold their breath'.

7. **Other language devices:** Although the poem is written in one long verse it can be seen as sets of five lines in which lines 4 & 5 rhyme, until the last five lines when it is lines 1 & 2 that rhyme. Short sentences heighten the tension: 'Don't breathe. Don't move. Stay dumb. Hide in your blindness'.
   Alliteration: 'sacks … smell like the seaside'; 'The dark damp smell of sand'.
   Onomatopoeia: The sounds are evoked by: 'whispering'; 'scuffle'; 'Push'.
   Enjambment: When the meaning flows from one line into the next: 'They'll probably be searching/The bushes near the swing.'

8. **Outcome/final impression(s):** We are left with the query: who had won? Were the older children being unkind in leaving the child 'unfound' – what would he feel when they laughed at him, when he had been so pleased with himself at hiding so well?

Collection B: Identity

'I Shall Paint My Nails Red' by Carole Satyamurti (answers to page 5)

'I Shall Paint My Nails Red' by Carole Satyamurti	
SUBJECT: A woman decides to assert her independence by painting her nails red. She considers the results of this deliberate gesture. Fortunately theeffects are 'reversible', not permanent.	**TONE:** Chatty; defiant. **VIEWPOINT:** The 'I' persona's view of the possible effects of her action.
USEFUL QUOTES: 'a bit of colour is a public service' 'I will look like a survivor' 'my lover will be surprised' 'it is reversible'.	**USE OF LANGUAGE:** No rhyme. A series of ten statements which explain the title; add humour; establish poet's personality. Repetition of 'Because' at the beginning of each line, gives a conversational feel; is defiantly ungrammatical. 'ten-minute moratorium': alliteration stresses quasi-legal authorisation to postpone/minimise consequences of actions.

'Digging' by Seamus Heaney (answers to page 7)

1   **What the title suggests:** Gardening? Growing things? Allotments?

2   **First idea:** As he sits at his desk, pen in hand, he hears his father digging outside, and looks down at him.

3   **Mood/tone created:**
Admiration of the physical prowess and skill of his father and grandfather.

4   **Later ideas:**
  - i   Looks at his forbears' past.
  - ii   His grandfather as champion turf cutter; a memory of taking him milk as he dug.
  - iii   Can't/ doesn't want to compete with his forbears at their skills.
  - iv   Decides he will 'dig' too, but with a pen not a spade (digging for truth?).

5   **Tension/conflict:** None, really.

6   **Imagery in use:** 'snug as a gun.'

7   **Other language devices:**
'gravely ground'
'buried the bright edge deep'
'tall tops; down and down.'
'curt cuts'
'the squelch and slap/Of soggy peat'
'Nicking and slicing neatly, heaving sods'.

8   **Outcome/final impression(s):**
He admires his forbears but is unable to follow in their footsteps as 'diggers' and turf-cutters; instead, he will 'dig' with his pen (into meaning/form). In a sense, therefore, he **is** following his ancestors!

Collection C: Nature

'The Thought-Fox' by Ted Hughes (answers to page 9)

'The Thought-Fox' by Ted Hughes	
SUBJECT: The poet is still at his desk at midnight, trying to write. In his imagination he sees a fox going out on the prowl and identifies with it.	**TONE:** Serious and speculative **VIEWPOINT:** The poet's lonely, bleak mood as he searches for inspiration is portrayed. The fox is wary and slow to emerge at first, providing a parallel with the poet's difficulty in filling a page.
USEFUL QUOTES: 'This blank page where my fingers move' 'warily a lame/Shadow lags by stump and in hollow/Of a body that is bold to come' 'a sudden sharp hot stink of fox'.	**USE OF LANGUAGE:** Very compact and dense, highly charged and metaphorical. No pure rhymes but achieves a pattern of sound through repetition and assonance. Powerful use of alliteration. A very sensuous poem – with examples of sight, sound, touch and smell.

'Keeping Orchids' by Jackie Kay (answers to page 11)

1 **What the title suggests:**
Bright, exotic flowers arising from rather bulbous (pregnant-looking) stems. 'Keeping' deliberately troubles reader, suggests either 'cultivation' (difficult in non-tropical regions) or 'possession' (impossible because flowers die).

2 **First idea:**
Deliberately vague and ambiguous: poet seems to have only recently met her mother for the first time – and been given some orchids by her, still in bud.

3 **Mood/tone created:**
We are disturbed, intrigued. The tone is mysterious, the mood depressing, sombre, eerie. There's something almost supernatural about the twice-breaking glass.

4 **Later ideas:**
i One of the buds has failed to open, presumably symbolic of the way her own life was not able to flower with her mother.
ii Poet is beginning to have difficulty remembering mother's face.
iii Mother had another daughter who died recently. Is this why mother has now met poet?
iv Poet goes over meeting with mother and suspects a life of deception.
v Poet suggests symbolically she will sever contact with mother.

5 **Tension/conflict:**
Natural tendency of a person to want to unite with birth-mother in conflict with resentment at having been abandoned.

6 **Imagery in use:**
A very deep, psychological poem which works through powerful images and symbols: 'Orchids', 'baby in a shawl', 'glass carafe', 'broken waters', 'digital watch', 'a bag of tricks', 'the draught in my winter room', 'cutting the stems with a sharp knife' etc.

7 **Other language devices: alliteration:**
'Her face is fading fast'
'A sad square, then a crumpled shape'
'So does/cutting the stems with a sharp knife'.

8 **Outcome/final impression(s):**
Nothing is certain in this poem, except the final feeling of emptiness. We sense, perhaps, that the poet has made a painful, fateful decision not to see her mother again.

The Media Non-fiction Texts

Language and Style (answers to page 19)

TITLE: 'Mind games' by Wendy Berliner
USE OF RESEARCH OR SURVEYS: Reference to 'US studies'; the project 'Fit to Succeed'; Governments SATS tests; 'A long-term French study'; QCA research findings; research by Sport England.
FACTS AND STATISTICS: The French study showed that where the school week was lengthened by 9.5 hours but teaching cut by 26% and limited to the morning, results were no worse.
JARGON/SPECIALISED VOCABULARY: 'dendrites – the slender filaments that branch out of the neurons'; 'we should be looking more holistically at education'; 'cardiovascular problems' etc.
USE OF EXPERT OPINION: Opinions of Susan Greenfield, Professor of Pharmacology; Steve Kibble, senior physical education director for Devon; Ben Tan, director of the British Heart Foundation.
EMOTIVE LANGUAGE/IMAGES: 'Couch potato kids'; 'children and teenagers idling their summers away in front of computer and TV screens'.
CAN YOU SPOT ANY BIAS? HOW STRONG IS IT? The writer appears to make a convincing case, based on expert opinion, of a correlation between physical activity and high levels of academic performance.

Different Cultures and Traditions

'A Stench of Kerosene' by Amrita Pritam (answers to page 24)

TITLE: 'A Stench of Kerosene' by Amrita Pritam Key theme: Love and marriage	
SECONDARY THEMES • Monogamy/polygamy. • Cultural need to have children. • Son and mother relationship.	
CAUSE OF CONFLICT	**WHO IS INVOLVED IN IT?**
Inability of Manak and Guleri to produce a child.	Manak and his mother.
Need for a second wife.	Manak and his mother; Manak and Guleri who love each other.
MORAL ATTITUDE OF A MAJOR CHARACTER Manak is faced with an impossible dilemma. He loves his wife and is happily married, but 'obedient to his mother and to custom'; he is forced to take a second wife to produce a child. Though he lacks the moral strength to go against his culture, after his wife's suicide his conscience forces him to reject the child of his second marriage.	
FIND A DIFFERENT CHARACTER WHO SHOWS A DIFFERENT MORAL STANDPOINT Manak's mother sees it as her religious and cultural duty to arrange for her son to take a second wife because he has failed to produce a child in seven years of marriage. She takes it on herself to pay 500 rupees for the second bride.	
THE MORAL ATTITUDE OF THE AUTHOR The author, writing about a practice that is now illegal, does not appear to judge or condemn. She writes in a spare and dispassionate style that allows readers to make their own judgements. However, the circumstances of the story, Guleri's suicide and Manak's suffering and rejection of the baby show where Amrita Pritam's sympathies lie.	

'The Schoolteacher's Guest' by Isabel Allende (answers to page 26)

Secondary Character: Riad Halabi

DETAILS OF APPEARANCE/POSITION ETC.
Turkish immigrant; most prosperous local shopkeeper; widowed and remarried; 65 years old but preserved his youthful vigour; had a reputation for being a just man.

ROLE IN STORY
Plays a supporting role, advising Ines, rallying the townspeople to her aid and organising the disposal of the body.

CHARACTER THROUGH ACTION

ACTION	WHAT IT TELLS US
i Consoled Ines when her son died; organised his funeral and calmed local people.	A level-headed person with leadership qualities.
ii Mobilises the townspeople to help Ines after she has killed the 'murderer'.	A good organiser, communicator and motivator.
iii Takes part in the removal of the body, uses his truck to transport it, assists with burial and says a prayer.	Is practical and prepared to be personally involved; has a strong sense of decency.

SIGNIFICANT THOUGHTS OR STATEMENTS
'The Lieutenant wouldn't understand that, Ines' (page 111).
'But that's not how the law works, Ines' (page 113).
'I'll take care of this in my own way' (page 121).

SUMMARY OF PERSONALITY AND MOTIVATION
A shrewd, practical, well-travelled, unflappable man, a natural leader who commands respect and has a strong sense of right and wrong.

Culture, Tradition, Atmosphere and Setting (answers to page 28)

Title	Place and period	Cultural issues
'Veronica'	Remote Nigerian village; 20th century.	Traditional role of the woman.
'The Schoolteacher's Guest'	Agua Santa.	Taking law into own hands to avenge 'murder'; bloodsports.
'The Gold Cadillac'	1950 Detroit.	Equality between the races; the beginnings of black prosperity.
	1950 Mississippi.	Racial prejudice and inequality.
'A Stench of Kerosene'	Chamba in Hindu district of Northern India, the Jammu and Kashmir region; mid-20th century.	Second marriage to produce a child.
'Vendetta'	Corsica and Sardinia in 1880s.	Blood feuds; the vendetta.

Comparing Stories (answers to page 30)

STORIES	'Country Lovers'	'Veronica'
Characters	Thebedi	Veronica

SIMILARITIES
Both girls are patient, trusting, uncomplaining and fatalistic – even though they have had hard lives in agricultural communities, and both love their child.

DIFFERENCES
Thebedi has the support of her family, who arrange a marriage for her, and neighbours; Veronica is beaten by her father as a girl, and is later alone in the world, before meeting her husband.

STORIES	'Veronica'	'A Stench of Kerosene'
Characters	A Nigerian village	A Northern Indian village

SIMILARITIES
Both are set in country villages, with strong agricultural roots.

DIFFERENCES
In 'Veronica' the natives work amongst the 'squalor' of village life in 'acute poverty'; in 'Kerosene' conditions are much better and the harvest is a time for festivity.

STORIES	'The Gold Cadillac'	'Country Lovers'
Theme	Racism	

SIMILARITIES
Two black girls receive painful lessons in racial prejudice. 'lois witnesses the harassment and indignity suffered by her father at the hands of white policemen. Thebedi has a relationship with a white farmer's son, resulting in a baby which the boy would rather kill than acknowledge. The white courts fail to find him guilty.

DIFFERENCES
The racial incidents are on wholly different levels. In 'Cadillac' the two races exist side by side with occasional conflicts between them. In 'Country Lovers' they are separated by Apartheid Laws – blacks only being admitted as servants.

STORIES	'Vendetta'	'The Schoolteacher's Guest'
Cultural issue	Blood revenge/the 'law of retaliation'	

SIMILARITIES
Corsica and Chile are both poor Catholic countries, where local people feel an obligation to disregard the due processes of law and seek personal retribution where the death of a kinsman is involved. Neither the widow Saverini nor Ines has a male relative and therefore personally assume responsibility.

DIFFERENCES
The Widow has no help in the community; whereas Ines discovers the entire community (including the Priest) is not only behind her but greatly excited by her action.

Answer to Quick Tip question on page 30

In one way or another all the stories have a common theme of some kind of threat to the community.

Media answers – Newspapers

Photographs (answers to page 34)

1 Comments might include: sequence by time or age of train to show progression and advancements in engineering.

2 Comments might include: different angles to enhance the power of the engine, speed of trains represented by blurring of image, static or action photos to show the relationship between the age of train and the development of photography.

Headlines (answers to page 34)

1. **Position:** Centred, under photos.	3. **Language:** 'tracks' literal and metaphorical, adds historical perspective and shows Eurostar following in the wake of its predecessors.
2. **Size:** Medium-sized.	4. **Information:** 'breaks British', alliteration for emphasis and memorability.

Content (answers to page 34)

1 The dates, names and speeds of the trains.

2 France.

3 20 minutes is cut off the journey to Paris.

4 The French 'locomotive Bo Bo passed the 200mph mark in 1955'; 'more sophisticated test version touched 322mph . . . in 1990, a feat that will remained unchallenged from this side of the Channel for a good while yet'; 'The Eurostar train, unlike renowned predecessors such as the Rocket and Mallard, owes more to overseas design than British. It is largely based on the French Trains Grand Vitesse.'

5 e.g. 'Britain becomes the fifth European country to joint the 300kph club . . .'; 'The driver of Train 3134, Alan Pears, said it was "very exciting"'.

Use of Language (answers to page 35)

1 Three: **what** 'the age of the high speed train'; **when** 'yesterday'; **where** 'Britain'.

2 'Roared', 'powering'.

3 They give the feeling of speed as they are verbs, and also the sound from the use of 'roaring', which is onomatopoeic. They are both quite dramatic words.

4 'Train 3144 reached 208mph (334.74kph) while pulling 14 cars'; '. . . their locomotive named Bo Bo passed the 200 mark in 1955'.

5 It shows the driver's feeling of pride in his achievement and adds immediacy to the article. It gives his **opinions**.

Writing to Analyse, Review, Comment

Writing to Analyse (answers to page 47)

Exam Practice Question

A suggested list of pros and cons for, 'The advantages and disadvantages of living in a city/large town'.

ADVANTAGES	DISADVANTAGES
1. More choice of housing.	1. More noise.
2. Better public transport.	2. More people.
3. Wider range of shops.	3. More traffic.
4. Better amenities.	4. More expensive housing.
5. More theatres, galleries and museums.	5. More crime.
6. Easier to get to other places.	6. Less privacy.
7. More jobs available.	7. More prone to terrorism.
8. Livelier than the country.	8. Bigger place to be lonely in.
9. More/better hospitals.	9. More impersonal.
10. Centre of business/finance.	10. Life goes at a faster pace.

Suggested opening paragraph:

Many people praise the countryside for being clean, quiet and relatively crime-free. Others say it is isolated, boring and lacks amenities, including public transport. Clearly there are two distinct views. The same may be said for the city: it is probably loved and hated in equal proportion.

Post-1914 Prose

Characters: Their Roles and Development in *To Kill a Mockingbird* (answers to page 53)

TEXT: *To Kill a Mockingbird*	Character: Scout

APPEARANCE
As Scout is the narrator she does not describe herself. Six years old. A tomboy, wears overalls not dresses . . . 'could not possibly hope to be a lady if (she) wore breeches'.

PERSONALITY
Lively, imaginative, trusting: believes 'was swapped' when born; **intelligent**: reads before going to school; **a leader**: 'You tell her Scout'; feels **kindly** towards Miss Caroline even when she has 'whipped' her; **witty**: describes Jem as 'in his old age'.
Sensitive/perceptive to feeling – before the jury returns to declare Tom Robinson guilty, she 'shivered', saying the 'atmosphere in the court room was exactly the same as a cold February morning'.

ROLE IN TEXT
As central narrator gives child's eye view of places, action, events, and other personalities.
Describes attitudes to: a) Boo Radley 'A malevolent phantom . . . people looked at the Radley Place unwilling to discard their initial suspicions.'
b) Racial prejudice: at school: 'buzzed with talk about Atticus's defence of Tom Robinson 'none of which was complimentary'; at home: 'Anything fit to say at this table is fit to say in front of Calpurnia.'
Influences events: as child speaks directly, 'Hey, Mr. Cunningham. How's your entailment getting along?' Her innocent remark breaks up men threatening Atticus outside jail.
Overall role: to show human capacity for good and evil and how understanding and sympathetic attitudes can mitigate against evil.

CHANGE AND DEVELOPMENT OF CHARACTER IN THE COURSE OF THE BOOK
At beginning **a child**, plays childish games, 'making Boo Radley come out'.
Learns from Calpurnia ' "that boy's yo' company and if he wants to eat up the table-cloth you let him, you hear?" '
Develops mainly through her father's influence, e.g. changes her attitude to Mrs. Dubose.
Matures in courtroom: 'Mayella must have been the loneliest person in the world'; through 'guilty' verdict on Tom Robinson. Decides 'it's not right to persecute anybody is it?'
At end has **adult reactions**, protects Boo, who has saved her, ' "It would be sort of like shootin' a mockingbird wouldn't it?" '

Relationships between Characters in *Of Mice and Men* (answers to page 54)

TEXT: *Of Mice and Men*	Characters: George and Lenny

AT THE BEGINNING OF THE BOOK
George, 'small and quick'; looks after Lenny, 'huge' and physically strong: '. . . for God's sake, don't drink so much . . . You gonne be sick like you was the other night.' Lennie dependent: 'Where are we goin', George?'
Lennie irritates George: 'So you forgot that awready, did you? I gotten tell you again, do I? Jesus Christ, you're a crazy bastard.'
Lennie sees relationship: 'I got you to look after me and you got me to look after you.' Their mutual dream: ' a little house . . . a couple of acres an' a cow and some pigs' where Lennie will 'tend the rabbits'.

IN THE MIDDLE OF THE BOOK
Relationship not so close. George plays cards with Whit, considers going to 'Suzy's'. Lennie tries 'not to attract attention'. George warns, 'If there is any fighting, Lennie, you keep out of it.'

AT THE END OF THE BOOK
Lennie accidentally kills girl. Remembers to 'Hide in the brush an' wait for George'. George anxious: 'Curley's gone want to shoot 'im . . .' George finds Lennie, re-tells story of 'dream', assures him that he's never been 'mad' at him; shoots Lennie, his hand shaking 'violently'.

Atmosphere and Setting in *Animal Farm* (answers to page 56)

TEXT: *Animal Farm*	
1 How does the writer create atmosphere at the beginning of the story?	The contrast between the disorganised humans (Mr Jones was 'too drunk' to shut up the farm properly) and organised animals who were full of expectation, as they sang of a 'golden future'.
2 How does the writer set the scene?	At 'Manor Farm' in big barn with raised platform. 'Majestic' Major addresses animals.
3 How does the writer show changes early in the story?	Animals preparing for 'Rebellion' – pigs in charge.
4 How do the characters respond to/help create the atmosphere?	Squealer: a talker could 'turn black into white' and expounded 'Animalism' to reluctant farm animals. Mr Jones 'disheartened', neglected his farm, which made rebellion 'easier than expected'. The following day the animals 'hurled' themselves into the air in their excitement, ecstatic at the fact that the farm was theirs.
5 How believable is the atmosphere created by the writer?	The hopes of the animals and the lack of enthusiasm of the humans make the situation possible and the atmosphere supports this.
6 Where else in the story does the atmosphere change?	**1** Atmosphere changes when the pigs set out '7 Commandments' for animals to obey and say harvest must take place more quickly than before. 'They toiled and sweated to get the hay in' but despite this the animals were 'happy'. **2** Snowball: disagreement with Napoleon over windmill. He set 'enormous dogs' on Snowball, who was 'seen no more'. **3** When Napoleon ordered slaughter of the four pigs and the animals became 'shaken and miserable' the animals 'crept back into the barn'. Napoleon took over.
7 What is the atmosphere at the end of the text and how has it changed from the beginning?	Hopeless (animals unable to distinguish pigs from men); their plight worse than at the beginning, when they were positive about the future.

1 How are the settings suitable for the story?	The farmyard setting with the barn for debates is ideal for the story.
2 Are there multiple settings? Give details:	Within the context of the farm, there are multiple settings; also the Public House (for humans). The barn, the windmill, the farmhouse, the fields, animal stalls.
3 What does the setting add:	
a) to our understanding of the characters?	The setting shows the hard work of the animals and the determination of Boxer, to his own detriment.
b) to the atmosphere?	At the beginning, when the farm is taken over by the animals an atmosphere of happiness is created, but as the pigs take over there is a gradual return to despondency and hopelessness on the part of the other animals.

Post-1914 Drama

Characters: Their Roles and Development in *Educating Rita* (answers to page 60)

TEXT: *Educating Rita* by Willy Russell	Character: Rita

APPEARANCE
Little obvious description but probably fashionably dressed, high heels, short skirts, bright colours. Age 26. Dyed blonde hair?

PERSONALITY
Bubbly, boisterous, lively. Very honest and direct ('D'y' need the money?' 'D'y get a lot like me?'). Swears (e.g. 'that stupid bleedin' handle'). Jokes ('Y' know Frank, Frank Ness, Elliot's brother?'). Quite witty.

ROLE IN TEXT
Central character, who wants to know 'Everything', via the Open University. She is the opposite of Frank in every way: he is drunk, disillusioned, a failed poet, husband and teacher. She is hungry to learn, change, live. She wants a 'choice' in life, to 'sing a better song', to have more possibilities than she started out with.

CHANGE AND DEVELOPMENT OF CHARACTER IN THE COURSE OF THE PLAY
Has already changed her name from Susan to Rita, and sees education as 'a better way of livin' me life'. She slowly learns **how** to study, read serious books, write academic essays. She eventually leaves her husband, passes her exams, changes her job, goes to the theatre, etc. She finds her voice, reverses the power balance between herself and Frank: 'I'm educated . . . I don't need you'.

Relationships between Characters: Arthur and Eric Birling in *An Inspector Calls* (answers to page 61)

TEXT: *An Inspector Calls*	Characters: Arthur and Eric Birling

AT THE BEGINNING OF THE PLAY/IN ACT 1
As Arthur lectures to the young couple, Eric crosses him twice: 'What about war?', 'Yes, I know – but still . . .' . Arthur snubs him: 'Just let me finish, Eric. You've a lot to learn yet.' Eric is critical: 'You've piled it [advice] on a bit . . . Father'. Simmering defiance in Eric, sharp speaking in Birling (e.g. 'You've had enough of that port, Eric.'). Eric quick to criticise/comment against Birling to Inspector, Birling quick to retaliate: 'Look – just you keep out of this'. Re-sacking of Eva, 'He could have kept her on instead of throwing her out. I call it tough luck.' (Birling: 'Rubbish!') Eric's outbursts: 'Well I think it's a dam' shame'. 'Why shouldn't they try for higher wages? . . I'd have let her stay'. Birling angry, Eric sulky/accusing. Eric on side of 'underdog', against his father.

IN THE MIDDLE OF THE PLAY/IN ACT 2
Birling tries, in vain, to persuade Eric to go to bed. Eric is off-stage for most of this Act. Birling refers to Eric as 'my boy' suggesting a) some fondness, b) a patronising attitude.

AT THE END OF THE PLAY/IN ACT 3
Birling 'explosively' refuses Eric a drink. Birling harshly critical of Eric and Daisy Renton and Eric resentful/critical of Birling's 'friends'; Birling attacks Eric about the £50 he stole and gave Daisy Renton; wants 'to cover this up'. Birling: 'Why didn't you come to me . . .?'
Eric: 'Because you're not the kind of father a chap could go to when he's in trouble, that's why.'
This shows they have never been close.

Atmosphere and Setting in *An Inspector Calls* (answers to page 63)

TEXT: *An Inspector Calls*	
1 How does the writer create the atmosphere at the beginning of the play?	The engagement party/toasts/speeches/the ring, etc. created an atmosphere of celebration and people being pleased with themselves.
2 How does the writer set the scene?	By the situation (above) and the conversation: upper-middle class business people, very respectable and aware of their own position and importance.
3 How does the writer show changes early in the play?	By the sudden arrival of the Inspector and his impact on the main characters, especially Birling and Sheila.
4 How do the characters respond to/help create the atmosphere?	Birling and the Inspector clearly have opposite views on things/people which introduces conflict. All the other characters are slowly drawn into it.
5 How believable is the atmosphere created by the writer?	Very believable: the tensions are soon clear.
6 Where else in the play does the atmosphere change?	During Sheila's interrogation; at the end of Act 1; during each character's 'confession'; after the Inspector leaves; during the two telephone calls in Act 3.
7 What is the atmosphere at the end of the text and how has it changed from the beginning?	Fear/anxiety/dismay; at the beginning they were all happy and carefree.

1 How are the settings suitable for the play?	In-period drawing room/servants, etc.
2 Are there multiple settings? Give details:	No. One room only.
3 What does the setting add:	
a) to our understanding of the characters?	They have the beliefs and attitudes of upper-class Edwardian England.
b) to the atmosphere?	A respectable setting adds to atmosphere of disrespectable revelations.

Literary Non-fiction

Does the Author Always Tell the Truth? (answers to page 65)

TEXT:
TRUTHFULNESS/OBJECTIVITY Much of the portrait of Grandpa in *Bad Blood*, for example, is based on the old man's own diaries.
EYE FOR DETAIL/POWERS OF OBSERVATION In Entry 11 of her diary, Anne Frank painstakingly describes the building and secret annexe, establishing the setting in great detail, at the outset.
SENSITIVITY/LITERARY ABILITY Adeline in *Chinese Cinderella* is an avid reader, and in particular a great lover of 'A Little Princess'; she wins the playwriting competition.

Characters: Their Roles and Development in *Bad Blood* (answers to page 67)

TEXT: *Bad Blood* — Character: Grandpa
APPEARANCE Not too much detail. He is described as 'thin and leathery'; 'lean and wiry'; and generally having a 'cynical expression'.
PERSONALITY As a young priest in the Rhondda he is depressed/disillusioned: 'He had learned to live with hopelessness'. He led 'a pottering, Pooterish, almost farcically domesticated life'. He is not a very devoted priest, on one occasion 'pretending to have been called away in order to escape parish business'. He is a complex character, preferring a quiet solitary existence, smoking his pipe or listening to the radio, rather than being actively involved with his flock. He appears full of self-doubt; 'self-absorbed and self-repelled at once, and the pottering alternates with bleak vistas of pointlessness'.
ROLE IN TEXT As an unlikely vicar, very poor, unhappy and 'ill-matched to Hilda'. He is intriguing to both his grand-daughter, the author, and to the reader.
CHANGE AND DEVELOPMENT OF CHARACTER IN THE COURSE OF THE BOOK After getting the living of Hanmer, a sort of promotion, he loses his long-term depression and has a 'resurrection of his ambitions and energies'. He becomes more outgoing, acquiring a bicycle and exploring his new district and having an affair with Nurse Burgess. He now lives a 'double life' which keeps him 'idyllically busy'. However, eventually he returns to misery, 'but of an altogether different order from the old dull depression'. He seeks consolation in putting on church pantomimes and gardening, trying to disentangle himself from the Nurse. He becomes debauched, miserably 'contemplating the waste of his talents': 'womanising became a routine vice . . . and he added booze to the last of his bad habits'.

Characters: Their Roles and Development in *The Diary of Anne Frank* (answers to page 68)

Relationships between characters

TITLE: *The Diary of Anne Frank*   Characters: Anne and her father

AT THE BEGINNING OF THE BOOK

Very much a 'Daddy's girl', happiest in his company, pleased by the postcards he bought her, having lessons with him; and admiring the patient, friendly way he talks Peter round and deals with all issues. She even goes as far as to tell, 'Daddy I'm much more fond of him than Mummy'. Later she says 'I adore Daddy. He is the one I look up to. I don't love anyone in the world but him'.

LATER IN THE BOOK

She begins to question his judgement and is miserable, feeling he shows favouritism to Margot: 'It wasn't right of Daddy to judge without knowing what the squabble was about'. She includes her father in a list of people she wishes would leave her alone; feels he is judging her over her deteriorating relationship with her mother.

AT THE END OF THE BOOK

No longer 'so affectionate to Daddy'; seeks independence 'to decide just a few things for herself'. Disregards his wishes she should not go upstairs to Peter's room. Feels she's come of age and resents parental influence, being 'able to live entirely on my own'. Later as a 'modern young girl', she is critical of him: 'he was never any support for me in my struggle'; always misunderstanding her.

Feelings and Emotions (answers to page 71)

TEXT: *Down and Out in Paris and London*   by George Orwell

Orwell in *Down and Out in Paris and London* describes a night at a 'Spike', a hostel for the homeless unemployed.

FEAR/FOREBODING

'When my cell companion stripped I saw that his chest was red raw, and, having spent the night a few inches away from him, I fell into a panic about smallpox.'

HUNGER

'Each man's ration was a half-pound wedge of bread smeared with margarine and a pint of bitter sugarless cocoa in a tin bottle.'

COLD/DAMP

'Naked and shivering, we lined up in the passage.'

OTHERS

Disgust: 'The scene in the bathroom was extraordinarily repulsive ... I shall never forget the reek of dirty feet ... Many men had to bathe in water where others had washed their feet.'

Alliteration: the repetition within a few words of the same consonant sound, especially at the beginning of consecutive words e.g. 'he is suddenly standing, silently' (from 'Miracle on St. David's Day' by Gillian Clarke).

Aside: words spoken by a character on stage, heard by the audience but not by other characters present; a convention to inform the audience what a character is thinking, for example the Friar in *Romeo and Juliet* saying 'I would I knew not why it should be slowed' when thinking of the haste with which wedding between Juliet and Paris is being planned (Act IV, Scene I, line 14).

Characterisation: the ways writers create characters, using physical details and personal qualities.

Climax: the height or pitch of excitement in a novel, short story or play.

Dramatic irony: this is when the irony of something that is happening is understood by the audience but not by some, or all, of the characters present, e.g. in *Romeo and Juliet* when Paris greets Juliet: 'Happily met, my lady and my wife' (Act IV, Scene I, line 18).

Exposition: the opening scenes of a play (or work of fiction) that 'exposes' i.e. introduces the characters, setting and plot threads.

Hyperbole: Deliberate exaggeration for the sake of effect.

Imagery: words and phrases that paint pictures in the reader's mind, often to suggest tone or emotion, and using similes or metaphors.

Irony: the use of words that imply something quite different from, and often quite opposite to, the literal meaning of what is being said.

Metaphor: a figure of speech which transfers the qualities of one thing to something else which are not normally thought similar e.g. 'The bushes hold their breath' (from 'Hide and Seek' by Vernon Scannell).

Mood: the atmosphere created in a poem or passage, not to be confused with tone, which is the author's attitude.

Narrator: the person or 'voice' telling the story. First person narration is when a character tells the story in his own words. Third person narration is when the author tells the story, describing the actions of all the characters.

Onomatopoeia: the use of words that sound like their meaning e.g. 'the **squelch** and **slap** of soggy peat' (from 'Digging' by Seamus Heaney).

Plot: the storyline or connected events in a work of fiction or a play.

Rhyme: corresponding or 'chiming' vowel sounds in words, used in poetry, especially at the end of lines.

Rhetorical question: a question posed to make a point rather than to receive an answer.

Setting: the place and period in which a story takes place.

Simile: a figure of speech in which something is described *as* or *like* something else e.g. 'darts like a tracer-bullet' (from 'Trout' by Seamus Heaney).

Soliloquy: 'the dialogue of the mind with itself'; a speech delivered by a character alone on the stage (or separated from other characters) as a means of sharing his or her thoughts with the audience. Juliet soliloquises at the beginning of Act II Scene V in *Romeo and Juliet*.

Structure: the means by which a poem or piece of prose has been put together in a coherent way, using verses, paragraphs, chapters, acts etc.

Symbols: a form of imagery where something symbolizes or represents something else. The orchids, for example, in 'Keeping Orchids' by Jackie Kay are an emblem for the poet of her mother.

Theme: the central unifying idea that runs through a piece of writing e.g. the idea of Fate and Coincidence in *Romeo and Juliet*.

Tone: the author's attitude to his or her own subject, for example humorous, cynical, bitter, serious, ironical etc.